A BENN STUDY · DRAMA

THE NEW MERMAIDS

A New Way to Pay Old Debts

THE NEW MERMAIDS

General Editors
BRIAN MORRIS
Principal, St. Davids University College, Lampeter
BRIAN GIBBONS
Professor of English, University of Leeds

A New Way to Pay Old Debts

PHILIP MASSINGER

Edited by T. W. CRAIK
Professor of English,
University of Durham

LONDON/ERNEST BENN LIMITED

NEW YORK/W. W. NORTON AND COMPANY INC.

First published in this form 1964
by Ernest Benn Limited
25 New Street Square, Fleet Street, London EC4A 3JA
Second impression 1981

© *Ernest Benn Limited 1964*

Published in the United States of America by
W. W. Norton and Company Inc.
500 Fifth Avenue, New York, N.Y. 10036

Distributed in Canada by
The General Publishing Company Limited · Toronto

Printed in Great Britain

British Library Cataloguing in Publication Data

Massinger, Philip
  A new way to pay old debts.—(The new mermaids)
  I. Title   II. Craik, T. W.   III. Series
  822'.3   PR2704.N3   80-42304

ISBN 0–510–34021–0
ISBN 0–393–90009–6 (U.S.A.)

CONTENTS

CONTENTS

ACKNOWLEDGEMENTS

A New Way to Pay Old Debts is a much-edited play, and I have not hesitated to draw upon the valuable explanatory notes of previous editors. I have consulted the editions of W. Gifford (London 1805; revised 1813, 1840), A. Symons (original 'Mermaid Series', London 1887), C. B. Wheeler (*Six Elizabethan Plays*, 'World's Classics Series', Oxford 1915), A. H. Cruickshank (Oxford 1926), H. Spencer (*Elizabethan Plays*, Boston 1933), M. St. C. Byrne (London 1949), P. Edwards and C. Gibson (*The Plays and Poems of Philip Massinger*, 5 vols, Oxford 1976) and C. Gibson (*The Selected Plays of Philip Massinger*, Cambridge 1978).

INTRODUCTION

THE AUTHOR

PHILIP MASSINGER WAS BORN at Salisbury in 1583 of a
Wiltshire family (the surname is often spelled Messenger). His father was employed in the household of
Henry Herbert, the Earl of Pembroke, at Wilton, his
office being that of house-steward and agent to the
Earl. Massinger was educated probably first at Salisbury
grammar school, and afterwards at Oxford, which he
left without a degree and for reasons unknown. By 1613
he was writing plays for the theatre-manager Henslowe,
to whom he applied for money when imprisoned with
two fellow-dramatists Daborne and Field for debt. It
is estimated that in some thirty years Massinger either
wrote or had a hand in some fifty-three plays. His
earliest collaborations and original plays were written
for the King's Men, the company of which Shakespeare had been a member and a writer, playing at the
Globe and Blackfriars theatres. John Fletcher had
succeeded Shakespeare as the King's Men's principal
dramatist, and it was Fletcher with whom Massinger
chiefly collaborated, Fletcher from whom he learnt
much of his dramatic art, and Fletcher whom he
succeeded in 1626 (after a short period of writing for
the Queen's Men, playing at the Cockpit, or, as it was
called when rebuilt after a fire, the Phoenix). He died
in 1640 and was buried in Fletcher's grave in Southwark Cathedral.

THE PLAY

1. DATE AND SOURCES

A New Way to Pay Old Debts was first published in 1633, the title-page stating that it had been acted by the Queen's Men at the Phoenix, a 'private theatre' in Drury Lane. No earlier reference to the play exists, and there is no record of its being licensed for performance. Its date of composition is accordingly unknown, and opinion is divided between those who place it in 1621 or 1622 and those who place it in 1625 or later. The later date is supported by Furnace's allusion to the siege of Breda (captured in May, 1625) in I.ii, a passage which does not look like an interpolation. There are no strong reasons in the content or style of the play, or in Massinger's circumstances as a dramatist, for preferring the early date.[1] A state of war, implied in Lord Lovell's campaign in the Low Countries, existed until peace was made with France in 1629 and with Spain in 1630. Sir Giles Mompesson the monopolist, glanced at in the name and character of Massinger's villain Sir Giles Overreach, was notorious from the time of his trial (in his absence, 1621) until much later.

The plot of the play is based on the main plot of Middleton's *A Trick to Catch the Old One* (printed in 1608), which supplied the stratagem by which a nephew regains his wealth from a cheating uncle, namely that of pretending that he is to marry a wealthy widow. The two plays are compared by Cruickshank (In Appendix I of his edition, Oxford, 1926), who shows that Massinger had read Middleton's play but had taken from it hardly anything but the outline of this situation.

In working up the situation for himself, Massinger introduces a second situation of his own, that of the

[1] Edwards and Gibson (*Plays and Poems*, II, 274–5) provide further topical support for 1625. See notes on V.i, 231–3, 395.

villain's daughter who contrives to marry the young man of her choice in spite of her father's opposition. This second situation, which is too closely linked with the first to be properly called a sub-plot, is treated by Massinger in a romantic spirit, and seems to have no direct source, though it is a situation on which many plays and parts of plays have been based.

An argument against dating the play in 1621 or 1622 is that Sir Giles Overreach has taken little from Sir Giles Mompesson besides his Christian name. Mompesson's prime offence was that he abused his monopoly of tavern-licences, mainly by charging exorbitant fees and by exacting bribes from the licensees. Overreach, however, is the traditional figure of the 'cruel extortioner' or 'cormorant', grasping at the lands of the needy and the improvident. Only in his power over Tapwell—a very minor aspect of the play—does he bear any topical resemblance to Mompesson. As for Greedy, his agent and catspaw, in whom Mompesson's confederate Sir Francis Michell has been seen, he is in the play as a figure of fun, not as an object of satire; and it is more likely that Massinger invented Greedy's connexion with Sir Giles as justification for bringing him into the play than that he invented Greedy in order to bring Michell into further contempt.

2. THE NATURE OF THE PLAY

The title-page describes *A New Way to Pay Old Debts* as a comedy, and the comedy is mingled of various kinds. The dominance of Sir Giles, which has struck everyone who has either read or seen the play, may be compared with that of Shylock in *The Merchant of Venice*; and Massinger seems to have been more conscious than was Shakespeare that the audience's strong interest could not survive the villain's fall. Accordingly he makes this fall conclude his play; a fact which, together with a succession of great actors in the part,[1]

[1] R. H. Ball, *The Amazing Career of Sir Giles Overreach*, 1939, gives an excellent record of the absorbing stage history, with full quotations from contemporary reviews by Hazlitt and others: these provide some of the best criticism that the play has received.

has emphasized what may be called the play's melo-dramatic quality. This quality is intensified by Massin-ger's tendency to moralize, and to comment on Sir Giles's wickedness through the words of the other characters and of the villain himself.

In this sense, then, the 'comedy' is the happy ending produced when a villain's plans are frustrated and the virtuous prosper. The characters for whom Massinger seeks and engages most sympathy are the young lovers, Alworth and Margaret. In them, particularly in Alworth, the predominant quality is a romantic and Fletcherian pathos. Though they have to play their part in defeating Sir Giles, they play it without gusto; they are passive rather than active beings, the stuff of which martyred lovers are made.[1] Welborne, whose stratagem gives the play its title, is a more spirited intriguer, seen at his best in the incidents where he handles Marrall and his uncle, and outbids Tapwell with Greedy. Yet Massinger does not appear altogether to have made up his mind about Welborne: he has had a prodigal past and numbers a surgeon among his creditors, but his speech that recommends him to Lady Alworth is a model of gentlemanly sensibility, and at the end of the play he redeems his reputation by accept-ing a military commission. He is far from the hero of Middleton's comedy, the adventurer Witgood; nearer to Charles Surface, the prodigal of generous impulses and genuine refinement, in *The School for Scandal*.

The whole comedy, in short, takes a sober colouring from Massinger's mind. But the conduct of the action is vivacious, with plenty of light incidental comedy in which the servants, Marrall, and especially Greedy have their important place, and with a constant and pleasurable excitement as Sir Giles's bustling villainy drives him forward confidently to his disaster. The play is pre-eminently a vigorous comedy of situation, and that it acts so well is not simply owing to the theatrical force of Sir Giles's character.

[1] Except the moments when Sir Giles succeeds in striking fire out of Margaret: III.ii.126; IV.iii.86.

3. THE DRAMATIC ACTION

Act I. The play opens with the hero at the lowest ebb of his fortunes, 'vomited out of an alehouse' in absolute beggary, the consequence of his prodigal career, and this opening scene closes with his resolution to restore himself. It sets both Welborne's and Alworth's stories moving, and is very obviously an exposition of situation and of character, but not an undramatic one: Tapwell's narrative is driven along by the vigour of self-satisfied malice, and Alworth's love for Overreach's daughter Margaret is unmasked instead of being merely discussed; Welborne is allowed to engage our sympathy not only by telling facts about himself (how he set up the ungrateful innkeeper, how he befriended Alworth's father) but by showing a practical interest in Alworth's affairs and by punishing Tapwell as he deserves.

After this introduction to the hero, we fix with surprise on Lady Alworth's particular advice to her stepson in the next scene:

And from one man I warn you, and that's Welborne:
Not 'cause he's poor, that rather claims your pity,
But that he's in his manners so debauch'd,
And hath to vicious courses sold himself.

These lines stand out from their context of sound but conventional advice (which itself, however, expresses the true nobility associated in the play with Lady Alworth and the soldier Lord Lovell, the ideal gentility of these two being contrasted with the brutal materialism of the upstart Overreach); and they point forward to Lady Alworth's encounter with Welborne in the scene which follows. Meanwhile, the dialogue of the lady's servants introduces the comic arrival of Greedy; and under cover of Greedy's absurdity, Overreach himself is brought in. Overreach might have burst into the play with a malevolent soliloquy. Instead, more subtly, he is given little part in the scene, but a decisive part; he silences Greedy with his curt

You know we cannot,

and indicates their relationship by the emphasis of

Will you lose me a thousand pounds for a dinner?

while his threat to his nephew displays his unnatural and savage character:

Thou art no blood of mine. Avaunt thou beggar!
If ever thou presume to own me more,
I'll have thee cag'd, and whipp'd.

This vindictive rejection (uttering which, Sir Giles flings out) is followed by Welborne's contemptuous rejection by the servants, his reluctant rejection by Alworth, and his indignant rejection by Lady Alworth.

The dialogue between Welborne and the lady is a minor crisis of the play: his fortunes begin to look up as his persuasive speech overcomes Lady Alworth; and when he declines her offer of money, just as he has earlier declined her stepson's, asking only for some small favour ('which you deny not / To strangers'), it is clear that he has a 'project' for re-establishing himself. This situation, with our consequent expectation of seeing his project in practice, ends the first act.[1]

Act II begins with Overreach, Welborne's adversary, returning in triumph from one ill-gotten legal victory and plotting others. His agent Marrall acts as a flattering confidant, allowing Sir Giles to expound his principles of worldly wisdom as well as his designs to complete his nephew's ruin and to marry his daughter into the peerage. Sir Giles complacently portrays himself as a monster of implacability and arrogance. He commissions Marrall, who is agent as well as confidant, to get Welborne to hang or drown himself; and the

[1] Massinger has been blamed for making Welborne whisper his request to Lady Alworth, as though it were done merely to keep the audience in suspense and ignorance. That is itself a sound theatrical reason for doing it, but a stronger reason is that a sleight-of-hand has to be performed here. The later action shows that Welborne has asked Lady Alworth not only to receive him socially but to pretend love to him; and this would be a very unseasonable request just after his praise of her and her late husband, praise which has raised both her character and his own in our eyes. No possible dialogue between them could have properly expressed it. It is thus better, in every way, that we should here guess what Welborne says, and later forget that he never announced his plan to Lady Alworth.

plot advances as Welborne, far from yielding to despair, makes boast of his hopefulness by inviting the incredulous Marrall to dine with him at Lady Alworth's, where they arrive in the next scene. Alworth's leave-taking of the servants conveniently bridges the gap, and also allows him to greet Welborne and make amends for his earlier coolness. The whole incident of the invitation to dinner, with the mystified servants diligently obeying orders and treating the ragged prodigal with the utmost respect (well contrasted with their barely suppressed ridicule of the vulgar and awkward Marrall), is full of dramatic life. Welborne's project is delicately revealed by degrees, and is never forced upon us by such devices as the soliloquy. Furthermore, Massinger, far from being restricted to working out the plot and displaying the main characters, allows Marrall to develop a comic personality of his own in this scene and the following one. Accompanying Welborne away from Lady Alworth's, he is farcically obsequious, and offers money and a horse so that Welborne may appear more like 'his worship'. But Welborne (who, as we can guess, is angling for a much bigger fish) rejects the offers, as he has rejected those of Alworth and the lady, giving a plausible enough reason for his behaviour. As soon as he has gone, Marrall, in a short but important soliloquy, reverts to his baser nature:

> well, well, Master Welborne,
> You are of a sweet nature, and fit again to be cheated:
> Which, if the fates please, when you are possess'd
> Of the land, and lady, you sans question shall be.

For with Overreach's entry, Marrall must become the villain's villainous confidant once more (he learns, and we do, that Lord Lovell is coming to dinner and that Margaret is to be set on to ensnare him); and his unexpected account of Welborne's good fortune, enraging his employer, shows Sir Giles in a comic light and promises greater annoyances to come, while Marrall's resentment of Sir Giles's anger and blows foreshadows his own disloyalty towards the end of the play.

Act III. Lord Lovell, whose visit Overreach has announced to Marrall at the end of the second act, opens
the third. On the way to Sir Giles's house, he holds an
idealistic dialogue with Alworth (who has just avowed,
off stage, his love for Margaret, and his fears that he
will lose her to his master). Nobleman and page vie
with each other in self-sacrifice. Lord Lovell swears on
his honour not to fall in love with the yet unseen Margaret. Alworth, maintaining that human nature is
incapable of resisting her beauty seconded by the
wealth of her father, releases his master from this
impossible undertaking and resigns himself to a life-
time of patient smiling at grief:

'Tis happiness, enough, for me to serve you,
And sometimes with chaste eyes to look upon her.

The rich sentiment of this scene is set off against
Overreach's two scenes which enclose it. He is busy
preparing for Lord Lovell. The material side of the
welcome, the banquet, he can entrust to Greedy, who
glories and luxuriates in his native element, the kitchen.
But the more important business must be Sir Giles's
own, and he calls in Margaret to instruct her in the
behaviour calculated to catch Lord Lovell. In their
powerful dialogue, the unprincipled father and his
virtuous sensitive daughter reveal each other's moral
character. Margaret's situation demands our sympathy,
as her father alternately cajoles and threatens her into
following his will, and finally leaves her alone with the
unknown Lord Lovell. Yet his previous scene with her
lover has sufficiently established Lord Lovell's virtue,
and a few whispered sentences are enough to bring
them to an honourable agreement to deceive Sir Giles,
so that there is no danger that the scene will move us
too strongly. The comic mood of the play is also maintained by the beginning of a series of dramatic ironies
at Overreach's expense (his misunderstanding of their
whisperings; his recommendation of Alworth, Lord
Lovell's supposed go-between, to Margaret). It is
maintained also, in a heartier way, by Greedy's interruptions, which comically torment Overreach while he

instructs his daughter and again while he tries to eaves-drop upon her conversation with Lord Lovell.

As soon as Lord Lovell and Margaret have agreed (to a plan very different from Overreach's), the arrival of a coach brings Welborne back into the story. He is warmly introduced by Lady Alworth and hypocritically welcomed by the astonished Sir Giles, to the accompaniment of Marrall's jeering asides; and they go to dinner, where Overreach is convinced by Lady Alworth's conduct that she is in love with Welborne.[1] He therefore gives Welborne a thousand pounds to clear his debts, and speed his marriage, ostensibly 'out of love, and no ends else', but really in order to get Lady Alworth's estate, as he has already plotted in soliloquy:

> if she prove his,
> All that is hers is mine, as I will work him.

Consequently, though we have now seen Welborne's project accomplished, our attention is not allowed to slacken. It is now Sir Giles's project that interests us, and this is skilfully linked in the next scene with Margaret's marriage, his other project.

Act IV. It is evident, from Lord Lovell's dialogue with Alworth, that the lovers will succeed:

> What is blest
> With your good wish my lord, cannot but prosper.

Even Overreach unconsciously helps them by his eagerness to hurry on the match with the nobleman. This eagerness now motivates his frank boast to Lord Lovell that he can get Lady Alworth's lands for him, and his whole brazen revelation of his wickedness; and this revelation, in its turn, being overheard by Lady Alworth, prompts her conversation with Lord Lovell,

---

[1] Massinger handles the dinner skilfully. Greedy's ludicrous catastrophe, and Overreach's early rising from table, cover the dramatic time which the meal takes. More importantly, Overreach's soliloquy relieves Massinger of the need to show Lady Alworth's somewhat immodest behaviour towards Welborne: instead, the grossness of the description ('And sits on thorns, till she be private with him') attaches itself to the *speaker's* character.

in which those two innocent dissemblers mutually reveal their good intentions towards the lovers and Welborne, and their own courtship begins.

The scene in which Welborne rewards his patient creditors, and punishes Tapwell and Froth for their ingratitude, provides an interlude of social realism and of broad comedy (in the behaviour of Greedy) between the scenes that concern the young lovers. It also provides an opportunity of showing Welborne's new prosperity and dwelling on his 'new way / To pay his old debts', for which there will be no time in the dramatic last act. This last act, it is clear from Marrall's disclosures about the legal deed, will turn upon some discovery by which Welborne may complete his victory over his wicked uncle.[1] Meanwhile, to conclude the fourth act, the young lovers are dispatched to happiness. Their dialogue (the only one the play allows them) is in its refined sensibility the counterpart of Alworth's first conversation with Lord Lovell; it touches briefly, too, a similar note of pathetic sentiment, when Margaret says (of her father),

> Suppose the worst, that in his rage he kill me,
> A tear, or two, by you dropp'd on my hearse
> In sorrow for my fate, will call back life
> So far, as but to say that I die yours,
> I then shall rest in peace;

However, with '*Enter* Overreach *behind*', we return at once to dramatic irony in the manner of the third act, and the scene culminates in Sir Giles's over-confident soliloquy in which he foresees his avarice and ambition gratified.

Act V consists of a single long scene. Its opening, the engagement between Lord Lovell and Lady Alworth, occupies a weak and undramatic dialogue in which (as

---

[1] The whole business of the obliterated deed is an awkward contrivance. Massinger needs it to maintain our interest in Welborne's contest with Overreach, which otherwise would sink in importance while we followed the lovers' fortunes. He does what he can by introducing the subject here (admittedly very abruptly) and by stressing at every previous opportunity Marrall's hope of revenging Overreach's hard usage of him.

in Lady Alworth's first long speech to her son about
true soldierly valour) Massinger puts forward moral
ideas (here about marrying widows) that have no direct
bearing on the play. The best that can be said for it is
that it adequately fills the gap between Overreach's
security and his misgivings. From his entrance, Overreach dominates the stage entirely. His first reverse,
the discovery that his deed of purchase of Welborne's
lands is a blank, is accompanied by a violent quarrel
with his nephew, in which swords are drawn, and by
bitter recriminations with Marrall. The dramatic ten-
sion is excellently controlled, with dramatic irony con-
tributing both to the suspense of the scene and to the
comedy of the villain's frustration. Overreach's lines

> after these storms
> At length a calm appears. Welcome, most welcome:
> There's comfort in thy looks, is the deed done?
> Is my daughter married? Say but so my chaplain
> And I am tame

are the prelude to his most vehement display of passion.
The chaplain's

> Do a father's part, and say heav'n give 'em joy

is so utterly inappropriate as to make Sir Giles both
ridiculous and terrible, gull and monster at once, in his
rage. His final collapse is the real end of the dramatic
action. Such matters as the kicking-out of Marrall and
the setting-up of Welborne as a soldier and a gentleman
are fitted artfully into the pattern of the scene, and a
neat transition from dialogue to epilogue sets the whole
play in perspective as an accomplished theatrical
entertainment.

4. THE VERSE AND ITS SPEAKING

Massinger's style may be called 'the middle style' of
blank verse. Influenced chiefly by Jonson and by
Fletcher, it reflects ordinary conversation, and suits the
contemporary setting and social moral of the play. It
can be heightened on occasion, as it is for Alworth's
poetical rhapsody on the beauty of Margaret (III.i.
60–80), or for Overreach's violent statement of his

remorselessness (IV.i. 111–131): on these occasions
the imagery, which is usually subdued, is more con-
sciously elaborated and displayed. At times, with a line
like 'I write *nil ultra* to my proudest hopes' (IV.i. 103),
Massinger deliberately strikes the resonant note of
Marlowe. There are other times, it must be allowed,
when the verse seems little better than versified prose,
a vehicle for the expression of trite moral opinions, such
as Lady Alworth's summary of her husband's views on
the military life (I.ii. 99–114). But usually, when it
reflects a present mood instead of stating abstract
principles, it is capable of a natural and flexible delivery.
The pauses fall not mechanically but naturally; the
feminine endings move the speech forward, and throw
into relief the strong stresses of the masculine endings:

> *Overreach.* 'Twas for these good ends
> I made him a justice. He that bribes his belly,
> Is certain to command his soul.
>   *Marrall.* I wonder
> (Still with your licence) why, your worship having
> The power to put this thin-gut in commission,
> You are not in't yourself?
>   *Overreach.* Thou art a fool;
> In being out of office I am out of danger,
> Where if I were a justice, besides the trouble,
> I might, or out of wilfulness, or error,
> Run myself finely into a praemunire,
> And so become a prey to the informer.
> No, I'll have none of't; 'tis enough I keep
> Greedy at my devotion: so he serve
> My purposes, let him hang, or damn, I care not.
> Friendship is but a word.
>   *Marrall.* You are all wisdom.
>   *Overreach.* I would be worldly wise, for the other
>   wisdom
> That does prescribe us a well-govern'd life,
> And to do right to others, as ourselves,
> I value not an atom.
>   (II.i, 8–26)

Phrases are taken up conversationally, as Overreach
here takes up Marrall's 'You are all wisdom' with 'I
would be worldly wise'.

Massinger is at his best in dialogue, as when Marrall, assiduously toadying to Welborne, produces twenty pounds

Which, out of my true love I presently
Lay down at your worship's feet: 'twill serve to buy you
A riding suit.
    Welborne. But where's the horse?
    Marrall. My gelding
Is at your service: nay, you shall ride me
Before your worship shall be put to the trouble
To walk afoot.
(II.iii, 30–35)

Welborne's dry query, and Marrall's self-appreciating wit in 'Nay, you shall ride me', are brought out by the metre. Upon Welborne's exit, the free rhythm of Marrall's soliloquy keeps pace with his bewildered and bustling thoughts:

How was I cozen'd in the calculation
Of this man's fortune, my master cozen'd too,
Whose pupil I am in the art of undoing men,
For that is our profession; well, well, Master Welborne,
You are of a sweet nature, and fit again to be cheated:
Which, if the fates please, when you are possess'd
Of the land, and lady, you sans question shall be.
I'll presently think of the means.
(II.iii, 53–60)

Likewise, at the climax of the play, the hurrying verse reflects Overreach's feverish excitement:

        Instantly be here?
To my wish, to my wish, now you that plot against me,
And hop'd to trip my heels up; that contemn'd me;
Think on't and tremble, they come I hear the music.
A lane there for my lord.
    Welborne. This sudden heat
May yet be cool'd sir.
    Overreach. Make way there for my lord.
(V.i, 257–62)

His repetition of his command—he does not even hear Welborne's warning, so powerfully is triumphant anticipation now working upon him—shows how well Massinger can embody character in verse.

A NEW WAY TO PAY

OLD DEBTS

A COMOEDIE

*As it hath beene often acted at the Phœ-
nix in Drury-Lane, by the Queenes
Maiesties seruants.*

The Author.

PHILIP MASSINGER.

LONDON,
Printed by *E. P.* for *Henry Seyle*, dwelling in S.
Pauls Church-yard, at the signe of the
Tygers head. Anno. M. DC.
XXXIII.

To the Right Honourable
ROBERT
EARL OF CAERNARVON,
Master Falconer of England

My Good Lord,

Pardon I beseech you my boldness, in presuming to shelter this comedy under the wings of your Lordship's favour, and protection. I am not ignorant (having never yet deserv'd you in my service) that it cannot but meet with a severe construction, if in the clemency of your noble disposition, you fashion not a better defence for me, than I can fancy for myself. All I can allege is, that divers Italian Princes, and lords of eminent rank in England, have not disdain'd to receive, and read poems of this nature, nor am I wholly lost in my hopes, but that your Honour (who have ever expressed yourself a favourer, and friend to the Muses) may vouchsafe, in your gracious acceptance of this trifle, to give me encouragement, to present you with some labour'd work, and of a higher strain hereafter. I was born a devoted servant, to the thrice noble family of your incomparable Lady, and am most ambitious, but with a becoming distance, to be known to your Lordship, which if you please to admit, I shall embrace it as a bounty, that while I live shall oblige me to acknowledge you for my noble patron, and profess myself to be

> Your Honour's true servant
> Phillip Massinger.

TO THE INGENIOUS
AUTHOR MASTER
PHILIP MASSINGER
ON HIS COMEDY
called *A New Way to Pay Old Debts*

'Tis a rare charity, and thou couldst not
So proper to the time have found a plot:
Yet whilst you teach to pay, you lend: the age
We wretches live in, that to come, the stage,
5   The thronged audience that was thither brought
Invited by your fame, and to be taught
This lesson. All are grown indebted more,
And when they look for freedom run in score.
It was a cruel courtesy to call
10   In hope of liberty, and then, enthrall.
The nobles are your bondmen, gentry, and
All besides those that did not understand.
They were no men of credit, bankrupts born,
Fit to be trusted with no stock but scorn.
15   You have more wisely credited to such,
That though they cannot pay, can value much.
I am your debtor too, but to my shame
Repay you nothing back, but your own fame.
Henry Moody, miles.

8 *run* ed. (Q ran)

4

To his friend the Author

You may remember how you chid me when
I rank'd you equal with those glorious men;
Beaumont, and Fletcher: if you love not praise
You must forbear the publishing of plays.
The crafty mazes of the cunning plot;   5
The polish'd phrase; the sweet expressions; got
Neither by theft, nor violence; the conceit
Fresh, and unsullied; all is of weight,
Able to make the captive reader know
I did but justice when I plac'd you so.   10
A shamefast blushing would become the brow
Of some weak virgin writer; we allow
To you a kind of pride; and there where most
Should blush at commendations, you should boast.
If any think I flatter, let him look   15
Off from my idle trifles on thy book.

                                        Thomas Jay, *miles.*

11 *shamefast* bashful
16 *Off* ed. (Q Of)

DRAMATIS PERSONAE

Lovell. An English Lord.
Sir Giles Overreach. A cruel extortioner.
Welborne. A prodigal.
Alworth. A young gentleman, page to Lord Lovell.
Greedy. A hungry Justice of Peace.
Marrall. A term-driver. A creature of Sir Giles
   Overreach.

Order.
Amble.
Furnace. ⎬ Servants to the Lady Alworth.
Watchall.
Will-do. A parson.
Tapwell. An alehouse keeper.
Three Creditors.
The Lady Alworth. A rich widow.
Margaret. Overreach his daughter.
Waiting Woman.
Chambermaid.
Froth. Tapwell's wife.

[Scene: Nottinghamshire.]

6

A NEW WAY
TO PAY OLD DEBTS

A COMEDY

Act I, Scene i

Enter WELBORNE, TAPWELL, FROTH.

Welborne. No booze? nor no tobacco?
Tapwell. Not a suck sir,
Nor the remainder of a single can
Left by a drunken porter, all night pall'd too.
    Froth. Not the dropping of the tap for your
        morning's draught, sir,
'Tis verity I assure you.
    Welborne. Verity, you brach!   5
The devil turn'd precisian? Rogue what am I?
    Tapwell. Troth durst I trust you with a looking
        glass,
To let you see your trim shape, you would quit me,
And take the name yourself.
    Welborne. How, dog?
    Tapwell. Even so, sir.
And I must tell you if you but advance   10
Your Plymouth cloak, you shall be soon instructed
There dwells, and within call, if it please your
        worship,
A potent monarch, call'd the constable,
That does command a citadel, call'd the stocks;
Whose guards are certain files of rusty billmen,   15
Such as with great dexterity will hale
Your tatter'd, lousy—

3 *pall'd* staled through standing
5 *brach* bitch   6 *precisian* puritan
8 *shape* costume   11 *Plymouth cloak* cudgel
15 *rusty billmen* watchmen armed with rusty bills

7

Welborne. Rascal, slave.

Froth. No rage, sir.

Tapwell. At his own peril; do not put yourself
In too much heat, there being no water near
20   To quench your thirst, and sure for other liquor,
As mighty ale, or beer, they are things I take it
You must no more remember, not in a dream sir.

    Welborne. Why thou unthankful villain dar'st thou
      talk thus?
Is not thy house, and all thou hast my gift?

    Tapwell. I find it not in chalk, and Timothy
25   Tapwell
Does keep no other register.

    Welborne. Am not I he
Whose riots fed, and cloth'd thee? Wert thou not
Born on my father's land, and proud to be
A drudge in his house?

    Tapwell. What I was sir, it skills not;
30 What you are is apparent. Now for a farewell,
Since you talk of father, in my hope it will torment
      you,
I'll briefly tell your story. Your dead father,
My quondam master, was a man of worship,
Old Sir John Welborne, justice of peace, and *quorum,*
35 And stood fair to be *custos rotulorum*;
Bare the whole sway of the shire; kept a great house;
Reliev'd the poor, and so forth; but he dying,
And the twelve hundred a year coming to you,
Late Master Francis, but now forlorn Welborne—

    Welborne. Slave, stop, or I shall lose myself.
40   *Froth.* Very hardly;
You cannot out of your way.

    Tapwell. But to my story.
You were then a lord of acres; the prime gallant;
And I your under-butler; note the change now.
You had a merry time of't. Hawks, and hounds,
45 With choice of running horses; mistresses
Of all sorts, and all sizes; yet so hot

25 *in chalk* on the score   29 *skills* matters
33 *quondam* former   39 *lose myself* go mad
41 *You cannot out of your way* You are a vagrant now

As their embraces made your lordships melt;
Which your uncle Sir Giles Overreach observing,
Resolving not to lose a drop of 'em,
On foolish mortgages, statutes, and bonds,   50
For a while suppli'd your looseness, and then left you.
    Welborne. Some curate hath penn'd this invective,
        mongrel,
And you have studied it.
    Tapwell. I have not done yet:
Your land gone, and your credit not worth a token,
You grew the common borrower, no man scap'd   55
Your paper-pellets, from the gentleman
To the beggars on high ways, that sold you switches
In your gallantry.
    Welborne. I shall switch your brains out.
    Tapwell. Where poor Tim Tapwell with a little
        stock,
Some forty pounds or so, bought a small cottage,   60
Humbled myself to marriage with my Froth here;
Gave entertainment.
    Welborne. Yes, to whores, and canters,
Clubbers by night.
    Tapwell. True, but they brought in profit,
And had a gift to pay for what they call'd for,
And stuck not like your mastership. The poor income   65
I glean'd from them, hath made me in my parish,
Thought worthy to be scavenger, and in time
May rise to be overseer of the poor;
Which if I do, on your petition Welborne,
I may allow you thirteen pence a quarter,   70
And you shall thank my worship.
    Welborne. Thus you dogbolt,
And thus.
                    Beats, and kicks him.

47 *lordships* estates
50 *statutes* bonds involving forfeiture in case of default
54 *token* tradesman's small 'coin'
56 *paper-pellets* promissory notes
62 *canters* rogues using slang   63 *clubbers* companions
67 *scavenger* official paid to clear streets of rubbish
68 *overseer of the poor* Poor Law guardian
71 *dogbolt* blunt arrow (contemptuous)

Tapwell. Cry out for help.

Welborne. Stir and thou diest:
Your potent prince the constable shall not save you.
Hear me ungrateful hell-hound; did not I
75 Make purses for you? Then you lick'd my boots,
And thought your holiday cloak too coarse to clean
      'em.
'Twas I that when I heard thee swear, if ever
Thou could'st arrive at forty pounds, thou would'st
Live like an emperor: 'twas I that gave it,
In ready gold. Deny this, wretch.
80   *Tapwell.* I must sir,
For from the tavern to the taphouse, all
On forfeiture of their licences stand bound,
Never to remember who their best guests were,
If they grew poor like you.
    Welborne. They are well rewarded
85 That beggar themselves to make such cuckolds rich.
Thou viper, thankless viper; impudent bawd!
But since you are grown forgetful, I will help
Your memory, and tread thee into mortar:
Not leave one bone unbroken.
    Tapwell. Oh.
    Froth. Ask mercy.

Enter ALWORTH.

Welborne. 'Twill not be granted.
90   *Alworth.* Hold, for my sake hold.
Deny me, Frank? they are not worth your anger.
    Welborne. For once thou hast redeem'd them from
        this sceptre:
But let 'em vanish, creeping on their knees,
And if they grumble, I revoke my pardon.
    Froth. This comes of your prating husband, you
95   presum'd
On your ambling wit, and must use your glib tongue
Though you are beaten lame for't.
    Tapwell. Patience Froth.
There's law to cure our bruises.
            [They go off on their hands, and knees.

75 *make purses* get business
92 *this sceptre* Q marginally explains, *His Cudgell*

Welborne. Sent to your mother?

Alworth. My lady, Frank, my patroness! my all!
She's such a mourner for my father's death,   100
And in her love to him, so favours me,
That I cannot pay too much observance to her.
There are few such stepdames.

Welborne. 'Tis a noble widow,
And keeps her reputation pure, and clear
From the least taint of infamy; her life   105
With the splendour of her actions leaves no tongue
To envy, or detraction. Prithee tell me;
Has she no suitors?

Alworth. Even the best of the shire, Frank,
My lord excepted. Such as sue, and send,
And send, and sue again, but to no purpose.   110
Their frequent visits have not gain'd her presence;
Yet she's so far from sullenness, and pride,
That I dare undertake you shall meet from her
A liberal entertainment. I can give you
A catalogue of her suitors' names.

Welborne. Forbear it,   115
While I give you good counsel. I am bound to it;
Thy father was my friend, and that affection
I bore to him, in right descends to thee;
Thou art a handsome, and a hopeful youth,
Nor will I have the least affront stick on thee,   120
If I with any danger can prevent it.

Alworth. I thank your noble care, but pray you in
        what
Do I run the hazard?

Welborne. Art thou not in love?
Put it not off with wonder.

Alworth. In love at my years?

Welborne. You think you walk in clouds, but are
        transparent.   125
I have heard all, and the choice that you have made;
And with my finger can point out the north star,
By which the loadstone of your folly's guided.
And to confirm this true, what think you of

125 *transparent* ed. (Q trans-/rent)
128 *loadstone* magnet of mariner's compass

130 Fair Margaret the only child and heir
Of cormorant Overreach? does it blush? and start,
To hear her only nam'd? blush at your want
Of wit, and reason.
Alworth. You are too bitter sir.
Welborne. Wounds of this nature are not to be
        cur'd
135 With balms, but corrosives. I must be plain:
Art thou scarce manumiz'd from the porter's lodge,
And yet sworn servant to the pantofle,
And dar'st thou dream of marriage? I fear
'Twill be concluded for impossible,
140 That there is now, nor e'er shall be hereafter,
A handsome page, or players' boy of fourteen,
But either loves a wench, or drabs love him;
Court-waiters not exempted.
Alworth. This is madness.
Howe'er you have discovered my intents,
145 You know my aims are lawful, and if ever
The queen of flowers, the glory of the spring,
The sweetest comfort to our smell, the rose
Sprang from an envious briar, I may infer
There's such disparity in their conditions,
150 Between the goddess of my soul, the daughter,
And the base churl her father.
Welborne. Grant this true
As I believe it; canst thou ever hope
To enjoy a quiet bed with her, whose father
Ruin'd thy state?
Alworth. And yours too.
Welborne. I confess it.
155 Tom I must tell you as a friend, and freely,
That where impossibilities are apparent,
'Tis indiscretion to nourish hopes.
Canst thou imagine (let not self-love blind thee)
That Sir Giles Overreach, that to make her great
160 In swelling titles, without touch of conscience,

131 *cormorant* greedy extortioner
136 *manumiz'd* manumitted, freed   137 *pantofle* slipper
141 *players' boy* actors' apprentice   142 *drabs* sluts
143 *court-waiters* court pages   155 *Tom*, ed. (Q True)

Will cut his neighbour's throat, and I hope his own
    too,
Will e'er consent to make her thine? Give o'er
And think of some course suitable to thy rank,
And prosper in it.
    Alworth. You have well advis'd me.
But in the mean time, you that are so studious   165
Of my affairs, wholly neglect your own.
Remember yourself, and in what plight you are.
    Welborne. No matter, no matter.
    Alworth. Yes, 'tis much material:
You know my fortune, and my means, yet something,
I can spare from myself, to help your wants.   170
    Welborne. How's this?
    Alworth. Nay be not angry. There's eight pieces
To put you in better fashion.
    Welborne. Money from thee?
From a boy? a stipendiary? one that lives
At the devotion of a stepmother,
And the uncertain favour of a lord?   175
I'll eat my arms first. Howsoe'er blind fortune
Hath spent the utmost of her malice on me;
Though I am vomited out of an alehouse,
And thus accoutred; know not where to eat,
Or drink, or sleep, but underneath this canopy;   180
Although I thank thee, I despise thy offer.
And as I in my madness broke my state,
Without th'assistance of another's brain,
In my right wits I'll piece it; at the worst
Die thus, and be forgotten.
    Alworth. A strange humour.   *[Exeunt.*   185

Act I, Scene ii

Enter ORDER, AMBLE, FURNACE, WATCHALL.

Order. Set all things right, or as my name is Order,
And by this staff of office that commands you;

171 *pieces* gold or silver coins	173 *stipendiary* dependant
180 *this canopy* the sky	182 *state* estate
184 *piece* repair	185 *humour* notion, behaviour
2 *staff of office* steward's white staff	

This chain, and double ruff, symbols of power;
Whoever misses in his function,
5   For one whole week makes forfeiture of his breakfast,
And privilege in the wine-cellar.
　　Amble. You are merry
Good master steward.
　　Furnace. Let him; I'll be angry.
　　Amble. Why fellow Furnace, 'tis not twelve o'clock
　　　　yet,
Nor dinner taking up, then 'tis allow'd
10   Cooks by their places may be choleric.
　　Furnace. You think you have spoke wisely
　　　　goodman Amble,
My lady's go-before.
　　Order. Nay, nay; no wrangling.
　　Furnace. Twit me with the authority of the
　　　　kitchen?
At all hours, and all places I'll be angry;
15   And thus provok'd, when I am at my prayers,
I will be angry.
　　Amble. There was no hurt meant.
　　Furnace. I am friends with thee, and yet I will be
　　　　angry.
　　Order. With whom?
　　Furnace. No matter whom: yet now I think on't
I am angry with my lady.
　　Watchall. Heaven forbid, man.
　　Order. What cause has she given thee?
20   *Furnace.* Cause enough master steward.
I was entertain'd by her to please her palate,
And till she forswore eating I perform'd it.
Now since our master, noble Alworth died,
Though I crack my brains to find out tempting
　　　　sauces,
25   And raise fortifications in the pastry,
Such as might serve for models in the Low-
　　　　Countries,
Which if they had been practised at Breda,

9 *taking up* being served upstairs
12 *go-before* gentleman usher
25 *pastry* room where pastry is made
27 *practised* ed. (Q practis'd)

Spinola might have thrown his cap at it, and ne'er
    took it—
  Amble. But you had wanted matter there to work
    on.
  Furnace. Matter? with six eggs, and a strike of
    rye-meal   30
I had kept the town, till doomsday, perhaps longer.
  Order. But, what's this to your pet against my lady?
  Furnace. What's this? Marry this, when I am three
    parts roasted,
And the fourth part parboil'd, to prepare her viands,
She keeps her chamber, dines with a panada,   35
Or water-gruel; my sweat never thought on.
  Order. But your art is seen in the dining-room.
  Furnace. By whom?
By such as pretend love to her, but come,
To feed upon her. Yet of all the harpies,
That do devour her, I am out of charity   40
With none so much, as the thin-gutted squire
That's stol'n into commission.
  Order. Justice Greedy?
  Furnace. The same, the same. Meat's cast away
    upon him,
It never thrives. He holds this paradox,
Who eats not well, can ne'er do justice well: 45
His stomach's as insatiate as the grave,
Or strumpets' ravenous appetites.
  Watchall. One knocks.

ALWORTH *knocks, and enters.*

  Order. Our late young master.
  Amble. Welcome, sir.
  Furnace. Your hand,
If you have a stomach, a cold bake-meat's ready.
  Order. His father's picture in little.
  Furnace. We are all your servants.   50
  Amble. In you he lives.

28 *took it*—ed. (Q tooke it.)   30 *strike* bushel
32 *pet* angry fit   34 *parboil'd* partly boiled
35 *keeps* stays in; *panada* boiled and flavoured bread pudding
50 *picture in little* miniature

Alworth. At once, my thanks to all.
This is yet some comfort. Is my lady stirring?

Enter the LADY ALWORTH, WAITING WOMAN,
        CHAMBERMAID.

Order. Her presence answer for us.
Lady. Sort those silks well.
I'll take the air alone.
        [*Exeunt* WAITING WOMAN, *and* CHAMBERMAID.
Furnace. You air, and air,
55 But will you never taste but spoonmeat more?
To what use serve I?
        Lady. Prithee be not angry,
I shall ere long: i'the mean time, there is gold
To buy thee aprons, and a summer suit.
        Furnace. I am appeas'd, and Furnace now grows
                cool.
60 *Lady.* And as I gave direction, if this morning
I am visited by any, entertain 'em
As heretofore: but say in my excuse
I am indispos'd.
        Order. I shall, madam.
        Lady. Do, and leave me.
Nay stay you Alworth.
        [*Exeunt* ORDER, AMBLE, FURNACE, WATCHALL.
        Alworth. I shall gladly grow here,
To wait on your commands.
65 *Lady.* So soon turn'd courtier?
        Alworth. Style not that courtship madam, which is
                duty,
Purchas'd on your part.
        Lady. Well, you shall o'ercome;
I'll not contend in words. How is it with
Your noble master?
        Alworth. Ever like himself;
70 No scruple lessen'd in the full weight of honour,
He did command me (pardon my presumption)
As his unworthy deputy to kiss
Your ladyship's fair hands.

53 *well.* ed. (Q well?)   55 *spoonmeat* soft food, pap
59 *cool* ed. (Q Cooke)   65 *courtier?* ed. (Q courtier.)

Lady. I am honour'd in
His favour to me. Does he hold his purpose
For the Low Countries?
    Alworth. Constantly good madam,   75
But he will in person first present his service.
    Lady. And how approve you of his course? you are
        yet,
Like virgin parchment capable of any
Inscription, vicious, or honourable.
I will not force your will, but leave you free   80
To your own election.
    Alworth. Any form you please,
I will put on: but might I make my choice
With humble emulation I would follow
The path my lord marks to me.
    Lady. 'Tis well answer'd,
And I commend your spirit: you had a father   85
(Bless'd be his memory) that some few hours
Before the will of heaven took him from me,
Who did commend you, by the dearest ties
Of perfect love between us, to my charge:
And therefore what I speak, you are bound to hear 90
With such respect, as if he liv'd in me.
He was my husband, and howe'er you are not
Son of my womb, you may be of my love,
Provided you deserve it.
    Alworth. I have found you
(Most honour'd madam) the best mother to me,   95
And with my utmost strengths of care, and service,
Will labour that you never may repent
Your bounties shower'd upon me.
    Lady. I much hope it.
These were your father's words. If e'er my son
Follow the war, tell him it is a school   100
Where all the principles tending to honour,
Are taught if truly followed: but for such
As repair thither, as a place, in which
They do presume they may with licence practise
Their lusts, and riots, they shall never merit   105
The noble name of soldiers. To dare boldly
In a fair cause, and for the country's safety

To run upon the cannon's mouth undaunted;
To obey their leaders, and shun mutinies;
110   To bear, with patience, the winter's cold,
And summer's scorching heat, and not to faint
When plenty of provision fails, with hunger,
Are the essential parts make up a soldier,
Not swearing, dice, or drinking.
  Alworth. There's no syllable
115   You speak, but is to me an oracle,
Which but to doubt, were impious.
  Lady. To conclude;
Beware ill company, for often men
Are like to those with whom they do converse,
And from one man I warn you, and that's Welborne:
120   Not 'cause he's poor, that rather claims your pity,
But that he's in his manners so debauch'd,
And hath to vicious courses sold himself.
'Tis true your father lov'd him, while he was
Worthy the loving, but if he had liv'd
125   To have seen him as he is, he had cast him off
As you must do.
  Alworth. I shall obey in all things.
  Lady. Follow me to my chamber, you shall
    have gold
To furnish you like my son, and still supplied,
As I hear from you.
  Alworth. I am still your creature. [*Exeunt.*

Act I, Scene iii

Enter OVERREACH, GREEDY, ORDER, AMBLE, FURNACE,
    WATCHALL, MARRALL.

  Greedy. Not to be seen?
  Overreach. Still cloister'd up? Her reason,
I hope assures her, though she make herself
Close prisoner ever for her husband's loss,
'Twill not recover him.
  Order. Sir, it is her will,

119 *warn* ed. (Q warn'd) **127** *Follow* ed. (Q You follow)

Which we that are her servants ought to serve it,   5
And not dispute. Howe'er, you are nobly welcome,
And if you please to stay, that you may think so,
There came not six days since from Hull, a pipe
Of rich canary, which shall spend itself
For my lady's honour.
    Greedy. Is it of the right race?   10
    Order. Yes, Master Greedy.
    Amble. How his mouth runs o'er!
    Furnace. I'll make it run, and run. Save your good
      worship.
    Greedy. Honest Master Cook, thy hand, again.
      How I love thee:
Are the good dishes still in being? speak boy.
    Furnace. If you have a mind to feed, there is a
      chine   15
Of beef well season'd.
    Greedy. Good!
    Furnace. A pheasant larded.
    Greedy. That I might now give thanks for't.
    Furnace. Other kickshaws.
Besides there came last night from the forest of
      Sherwood
The fattest stag I ever cook'd.
    Greedy. A stag man?
    Furnace. A stag sir, part of it prepar'd for dinner,   20
And bak'd in puffpaste.
    Greedy. Puffpaste too, Sir Giles!
A ponderous chine of beef! a pheasant larded!
And red deer too Sir Giles, and bak'd in puffpaste!
All business set aside; let us give thanks here.
    Furnace. How the lean skeleton's rapt!
    Overreach. You know we cannot.   25
    Marrall. Your worships are to sit on a commission,
And if you fail to come, you lose the cause.
    Greedy. Cause me no causes, I'll prove't, for such a
      dinner
We may put off a commission: you shall find it

8 *pipe* 126 gallons   10 *race* characteristic flavour
16 *larded* garnished with bacon   17 *kickshaws* delicacies
25 *rapt* ed. (Q rap'd) transported with joy

Henrici decimo quarto.

30   *Overreach.* Fie Master Greedy.
Will you lose me a thousand pounds for a dinner?
No more for shame. We must forget the belly,
When we think of profit.
     Greedy. Well, you shall o'errule me.
I could ev'n cry now. Do you hear Master Cook.
35 Send but a corner of that immortal pasty,
And I, in thankfulness, will by your boy
Send you a brace of threepences.
     Furnace. Will you be so prodigal?

Enter WELBORNE.

Overreach. Remember me to your lady. Who have
     we here?
Welborne. You know me.
Overreach. I did once, but now I will not,
40 Thou art no blood of mine. Avaunt thou beggar!
If ever thou presume to own me more,
I'll have thee cag'd, and whipp'd.
     Greedy. I'll grant the warrant.
Think of Pie-Corner, Furnace.
                    [*Exeunt* OVERREACH, GREEDY, MARRALL.
     Watchall. Will you out sir?
I wonder how you durst creep in.
     Order. This is rudeness,
And saucy impudence.
45   *Amble.* Cannot you stay
To be serv'd among your fellows from the basket,
But you must press into the hall?
     Furnace. Prithee vanish
Into some outhouse, though it be the pig-sty;
My scullion shall come to thee.

Enter ALWORTH.

Welborne. This is rare:
Oh here's Tom Alworth. Tom.
50   *Alworth.* We must be strangers,

46 *basket* of scraps given to the poor at the gate
48 *though* ed. (Q thought)
50 *Tom Alworth. Tom.* ed. (Q Tom. Alworth Tom).

Nor would I have you seen here for a million.

[*Exit* ALWORTH.

Welborne. Better and better. He contemns me too?

Enter WOMAN *and* CHAMBERMAID.

Woman. Foh what a smell's here! what thing's this?
Chambermaid. A creature
Made out of the privy. Let us hence for love's sake,
Or I shall swoon.
  Woman. I begin to faint already.   55

[*Exeunt* WOMAN *and* CHAMBERMAID.

Watchall. Will' know your way?
  Amble. Or shall we teach it you,
By the head, and shoulders?
  Welborne. No: I will not stir.
Do you mark, I will not. Let me see the wretch
That dares attempt to force me. Why you slaves,
Created only to make legs, and cringe;   60
To carry in a dish, and shift a trencher;
That have not souls only to hope a blessing
Beyond black jacks, or flagons; you that were born
Only to consume meat, and drink, and batten
Upon reversions: who advances? who   65
Shows me the way?
  Order. My lady.

Enter LADY, WOMAN, CHAMBERMAID.

Chambermaid. Here's the monster.
  Woman. Sweet madam, keep your glove to your
     nose.
  Chambermaid. Or let me
Fetch some perfumes may be predominant,
You wrong yourself else.
  Welborne. Madam, my designs
Bear me to you.
  Lady. To me?
  Welborne. And though I have met with   70
But ragged entertainment from your grooms here,

56 *Will' know* ed. (Q Will know)   60 *make legs* bow
63 *black jacks* leather beer-jugs
64–65 *batten upon reversions* grow fat on left-overs

I hope from you to receive that noble usage,
As may become the true friend of your husband,
And then I shall forget these—
    Lady. I am amaz'd,
75 To see, and hear this rudeness. Dar'st thou think
Though sworn, that it can ever find belief,
That I, who to the best men of this country,
Deni'd my presence since my husband's death,
Can fall so low, as to change words with thee?
80 Thou son of infamy, forbear my house,
And know, and keep the distance that's between us,
Or, though it be against my gentler temper,
I shall take order you no more shall be
An eye-sore to me.
    Welborne. Scorn me not good lady;
85 But as in form you are angelical
Imitate the heavenly natures, and vouchsafe
At the least awhile to hear me. You will grant
The blood that runs in this arm, is as noble
As that which fills your veins; those costly jewels,
And those rich clothes you wear; your men's
90   observance,
And women's flattery, are in you no virtues,
Nor these rags, with my poverty, in me vices.
You have a fair fame, and I know deserve it,
Yet lady I must say in nothing more,
95 Than in the pious sorrow you have shown
For your late noble husband.
    Order. How she starts!
    Furnace. And hardly can keep finger from the eye
To hear him nam'd.
    Lady. Have you ought else to say?
    Welborne. That husband madam, was once in his
      fortune
100 Almost as low, as I. Want, debts, and quarrels
Lay heavy on him: let it not be thought
A boast in me, though I say, I reliev'd him.
'Twas I that gave him fashion; mine the sword

74 *these—* ed. (Q these.)
97 *keep finger from the eye* refrain from weeping
103 *gave him fashion* raised him in society

That did on all occasions second his;
I brought him on, and off with honour, lady: 105
And when in all men's judgements he was sunk,
And in his own hopes not to be buoy'd up,
I stepp'd unto him, took him by the hand,
And set him upright.
   Furnace. Are not we base rogues
That could forget this?
   Welborne. I confess you made him   110
Master of your estate, nor could your friends
Though he brought no wealth with him blame you
     for't.
For he had a shape, and to that shape a mind
Made up of all parts, either great, or noble,
So winning a behaviour, not to be   115
Resisted, madam.
   Lady. 'Tis most true, he had.
   Welborne. For his sake then, in that I was his
     friend,
Do not contemn me.
   Lady. For what's past, excuse me,
I will redeem it. Order, give the gentleman
A hundred pounds.
   Welborne. No madam, on no terms: 120
I will nor beg, nor borrow six pence of you,
But be suppli'd elsewhere, or want thus ever.
Only one suit I make, which you deny not
To strangers: and 'tis this.
                    Whispers to her.
   Lady. Fie, nothing else?
   Welborne. Nothing; unless you please to charge
     your servants,   125
To throw away a little respect upon me.
   Lady. What you demand is yours.
   Welborne. I thank you, lady.
Now what can be wrought out of such a suit,
Is yet in supposition; I have said all,
When you please you may retire. [*Exit* LADY.] Nay,
     all's forgotten,   130
And for a lucky omen to my project,

107 *buoy'd up* ed. (Q bung'd up)   118 *contemn* scorn

Shake hands, and end all quarrels in the cellar.
Order. Agreed, agreed.
Furnace. Still merry Master Welborne.

[*Exeunt.*

Act II, Scene i

Enter OVERREACH, MARRALL.

Overreach. He's gone I warrant thee; this
     commission crush'd him.
Marrall. Your worship have the way on't, and
     ne'er miss
To squeeze these unthrifts into air: and yet
The chap-fall'n justice did his part, returning
5   For your advantage the certificate
Against his conscience, and his knowledge too,
(With your good favour) to the utter ruin
Of the poor farmer.
     Overreach. 'Twas for these good ends
I made him a justice. He that bribes his belly,
Is certain to command his soul.
10   *Marrall.* I wonder
(Still with your licence) why, your worship having
The power to put this thin-gut in commission,
You are not in't yourself?
     Overreach. Thou art a fool;
In being out of office I am out of danger,
15   Where if I were a justice, besides the trouble,
I might, or out of wilfulness, or error,
Run myself finely into a praemunire,
And so become a prey to the informer.
No, I'll have none of't; 'tis enough I keep
20   Greedy at my devotion: so he serve
My purposes, let him hang, or damn, I care not.
Friendship is but a word.
     Marrall. You are all wisdom.
     Overreach. I would be worldly wise, for the other
          wisdom

2 *on't* ed. (Q out)   4 *chap-fall'n* hollow-cheeked
5 *certificate* legal decision
17 *praemunire* liability to punishment by loss of property

That does prescribe us a well-govern'd life,
And to do right to others, as ourselves,   25
I value not an atom.
    Marrall. What course take you
(With your good patience) to hedge in the manor
Of your neighbour Master Frugal? as 'tis said,
He will nor sell, nor borrow, nor exchange,
And his land lying in the midst of your many
        lordships,   30
Is a foul blemish.
    Overreach. I have thought on't, Marrall,
And it shall take. I must have all men sellers,
And I the only purchaser.
    Marrall. 'Tis most fit sir.
    Overreach. I'll therefore buy some cottage near his
        manor,
Which done, I'll make my men break ope his fences;   35
Ride o'er his standing corn, and in the night
Set fire on his barns; or break his cattle's legs.
These trespasses draw on suits, and suits expenses,
Which I can spare, but will soon beggar him.
When I have harried him thus two, or three year,   40
Though he sue *in forma pauperis*, in spite
Of all his thrift, and care he'll grow behind-hand.
    Marrall. The best I ever heard; I could adore you.
    Overreach. Then with the favour of my man of law,
I will pretend some title: want will force him   45
To put it to arbitrement: then if he sell
For half the value, he shall have ready money,
And I possess his land.
    Marrall. 'Tis above wonder!
Welborne was apt to sell, and needed not
These fine arts sir to hook him in.
    Overreach. Well thought on.   50
This varlet Marrall lives too long, to upbraid me
With my close cheat put upon him. Will nor cold,

27 *hedge in* enclose to your own use
41 *sue in forma pauperis* bring actions without paying costs (as a
    poor man)
45 *pretend some title* put forward some claim
46 *put it to arbitrement* come to a compromise
52 *close cheat* secret fraud

Nor hunger kill him?
 Marrall. I know not what to think on't.
I have us'd all means, and the last night I caus'd
55 His host the tapster to turn him out of doors;
And have been since with all your friends, and
  tenants,
And on the forfeit of your favour charg'd them,
Though a crust of mouldy bread would keep him
  from starving,
Yet they should not relieve him. This is done, sir.
 Overreach. That was something, Marrall, but thou
60   must go further,
And suddenly Marrall.
 Marrall. Where, and when you please sir.
 Overreach. I would have thee seek him out, and if
  thou canst,
Persuade him that 'tis better steal, than beg.
Then if I prove he has but robb'd a henroost,
65 Not all the world shall save him from the gallows.
Do any thing to work him to despair,
And 'tis thy masterpiece.
 Marrall. I will do my best, sir.
 Overreach. I am now on my main work with the
  Lord Lovell,
The gallant minded, popular Lord Lovell;
70 The minion of the people's love. I hear
He's come into the country, and my aims are
To insinuate myself into his knowledge,
And then invite him to my house.
 Marrall. I have you.
This points at my young mistress.
 Overreach. She must part with
75 That humble title, and write honourable,
Right honourable Marrall, my right honourable
  daughter;
If all I have, or e'er shall get will do it.
I will have her well attended, there are ladies
Of errant knights decay'd, and brought so low,
80 That for cast clothes, and meat, will gladly serve her.

57 *charg'd them* ed. (Q charg'd him) 70 *minion* favourite, darling
71 *country* county, shire 79 *errant* (= arrant) undoubted

And 'tis my glory, though I come from the city,
To have their issue, whom I have undone,
To kneel to mine, as bond-slaves.
    Marrall. 'Tis fit state, sir.
    Overreach. And therefore, I'll not have a
        chambermaid
That ties her shoes, or any meaner office,   85
But such whose fathers were right worshipful.
'Tis a rich man's pride, there having ever been
More than a feud, a strange antipathy
Between us, and true gentry.

Enter WELBORNE.

    Marrall. See, who's here, sir.
    Overreach. Hence monster; prodigy!
    Welborne. Sir your wife's nephew;   90
She, and my father tumbled in one belly.
    Overreach. Avoid my sight, thy breath's infectious,
        rogue.
I shun thee as a leprosy, or the plague.
Come hither Marrall, this is the time to work him.
    Marrall. I warrant you, sir.   [*Exit* OVERREACH.
    Welborne. By this light I think he's mad.   95
    Marrall. Mad? had you took compassion on
        yourself,
You long since had been mad.
    Welborne. You have took a course
Between you, and my venerable uncle,
To make me so.
    Marrall. The more pale spirited you,
That would not be instructed. I swear deeply—   100
    Welborne. By what?
    Marrall. By my religion.
    Welborne. Thy religion!
The devil's creed, but what would you have done?
    Marrall. Had there been but one tree in all the
        shire,
Nor any hope to compass a penny halter,
Before, like you, I had outliv'd my fortunes,   105
A withe had serv'd my turn to hang myself.

100 *deeply*— ed. (Q deeply.)   106 *withe* flexible willow branch

I am zealous in your cause: pray you hang yourself,
And presently, as you love your credit.
    Welborne. I thank you.
    Marrall. Will you stay till you die in a ditch? or
        lice devour you?
110 Or if you dare not do the feat yourself,
But that you'll put the state to charge, and trouble,
Is there no purse to be cut? house to be broken?
Or market women with eggs that you may murder,
And so dispatch the business.
    Welborne. Here's variety
115 I must confess; but I'll accept of none
Of all your gentle offers, I assure you.
    Marrall. Why, have you hope ever to eat again?
Or drink? Or be the master of three farthings?
If you like not hanging, drown yourself, take some
        course
For your reputation.
120   *Welborne.* 'Twill not do; dear tempter,
With all the rhetoric the fiend hath taught you.
I am as far as thou art from despair,
Nay, I have confidence, which is more than hópe,
To live, and suddenly better than ever.
125   *Marrall.* Ha! ha! these castles you build in the air
Will not persuade me, or to give, or lend
A token to you.
    Welborne. I'll be more kind to thee.
Come thou shalt dine with me.
    Marrall. With you!
    Welborne. Nay more, dine gratis.
    Marrall. Under what hedge I pray you? Or at
        whose cost?
Are they padders? or abram-men, that are your
130   consorts?
    Welborne. Thou art incredulous, but thou shalt dine
Not alone at her house, but with a gallant lady,
With me, and with a lady.
    Marrall. Lady! what lady?

---

128 *With you!* ed. (Q With you.)   128 *gratis* free of charge
130 *padders* footpads; *abram-men* beggars pretending madness

With the Lady of the Lake, or Queen of Fairies?
For I know, it must be an enchanted dinner.   135
   Welborne. With the Lady Alworth, knave.
   Marrall. Nay, now there's hope
Thy brain is crack'd.
   Welborne. Mark there, with what respect
I am entertain'd.
   Marrall. With choice no doubt of dog-whips.
Why, dost thou ever hope to pass her porter?
   Welborne. 'Tis not far off, go with me: trust thine
      own eyes.   140
   Marrall. Troth in my hope, or my assurance rather
To see thee curvet, and mount like a dog in a blanket
If ever thou presume to pass her threshold,
I will endure thy company.
   Welborne. Come along then.   [*Exeunt.*

Act II, Scene ii

Enter ALWORTH, WAITING-WOMAN, CHAMBERMAID,
    ORDER, AMBLE, FURNACE, WATCHALL.

   Woman. Could you not command your leisure one
      hour longer?
   Chambermaid. Or half an hour?
   Alworth. I have told you what my haste is:
Besides being now another's, not mine own,
Howe'er I much desire to enjoy you longer,
My duty suffers, if to please myself   5
I should neglect my lord.
   Woman. Pray you do me the favour
To put these few quince-cakes into your pocket,
They are of mine own preserving.
   Chambermaid. And this marmalade;
'Tis comfortable for your stomach.
   Woman. And at parting
Excuse me if I beg a farewell from you.   10

134 *the Lady of the Lake* the enchantress of the *Morte d'Arthur*
142 *curvet* skip, leap (when tossed aloft)

Chambermaid. You are still before me. I move the
same suit sir.
Kisses 'em severally.
Furnace. How greedy these chamberers are of a
beardless chin!
I think the tits will ravish him.
Alworth. My service
To both.
Woman. Ours waits on you.
Chambermaid. And shall do ever.
Order. You hear my lady's charge, be therefore
15   careful
That you sustain your parts.
Woman. We can bear I warrant you.
[*Exeunt* WOMAN *and* CHAMBERMAID.
Furnace. Here; drink it off, the ingredients are
cordial,
And this the true elixir; it hath boil'd
Since midnight for you. 'Tis the quintessence
20   Of five cocks of the game, ten dozen of sparrows,
Knuckles of veal, potato roots, and marrow;
Coral, and ambergris: were you two years elder,
And I had a wife, or gamesome mistress,
I durst trust you with neither: you need not bait
25   After this I warrant you, though your journey's long,
You may ride on the strength of this till tomorrow
morning.
Alworth. Your courtesies overwhelm me: I much
grieve
To part from such true friends, and yet find comfort;
My attendance on my honourable lord
30   (Whose resolution holds to visit my lady)
Will speedily bring me back.
Knocking at the gate; MARRALL *and* WELBORNE
within.
Marrall. Dar'st thou venture further?

12 *chamberers* waiting-women   13 *think* ed. (Q thinne)
13 *tits* wenches   15 *hear* ed. (Q are)
18 *true elixir* genuine water of life
21 *potato roots* sweet potatoes
24 *bait* rest and eat on the journey

Welborne. Yes, yes, and knock again.

Order. 'Tis he; disperse.

Amble. Perform it bravely.

Furnace. I know my cue, ne'er doubt me.

                              [*They go off several ways.*

Watchall. Beast that I was to make you stay: most
        welcome,

You were long since expected.

Welborne. Say so much   35

To my friend I pray you.

Watchall. For your sake I will sir.

Marrall. For his sake!

Welborne. Mum; this is nothing.

Marrall. More than ever

I would have believ'd, though I had found it in my
        primer.

Alworth. When I have giv'n you reasons for my
        late harshness,

You'll pardon, and excuse me: for, believe me,   40

Though now I part abruptly, in my service

I will deserve it.

Marrall. Service! with a vengeance!

Welborne. I am satisfied: farewell Tom.

Alworth. All joy stay with you.

                       [*Exit* ALWORTH. *Enter* AMBLE.

Amble. You are happily encounter'd: I yet never

Presented one so welcome, as I know   45

You will be to my lady.

Marrall. This is some vision;

Or sure these men are mad, to worship a dunghill;

It cannot be a truth.

Welborne. Be still a pagan,

An unbelieving infidel, be so miscreant,

And meditate on blankets, and on dog-whips.   50

Enter FURNACE.

Furnace. I am glad you are come, until I know your
        pleasure,

I knew not how to serve up my lady's dinner.

Marrall. His pleasure; is it possible?

38 *primer* prayer-book

Welborne. What's thy will?

Furnace. Marry sir, I have some grouse, and
          turkey chicken,
Some rails, and quails, and my lady will'd me ask
55   you
What kind of sauces best affect your palate,
That I may use my utmost skill to please it.

          Marrall. The devil's enter'd this cook, sauce for
          his palate!
That on my knowledge, for almost this twelve month
60   Durst wish but cheeseparings, and brown bread on
          Sundays.

          Welborne. That way I like 'em best.

          Furnace. It shall be done sir.   [*Exit* FURNACE.

          Welborne. What think you of the hedge we shall
          dine under?
Shall we feed gratis?

          Marrall. I know not what to think;
Pray you make me not mad.

Enter ORDER.

Order. This place becomes you not;
Pray you walk sir, to the dining room.

65   *Welborne.* I am well here
Till her ladyship quits her chamber.

          Marrall. Well here say you?
'Tis a rare change! but yesterday you thought
Yourself well in a barn, wrapp'd up in pease-straw.

Enter WOMAN, *and* CHAMBERMAID.

Woman. O sir, you are wish'd for.

          Chambermaid. My lady dreamt sir of you.

          Woman. And the first command she gave, after she
70   rose,
Was (her devotions done) to give her notice
When you approach'd here.

          Chambermaid. Which is done on my virtue.

          Marrall. I shall be converted, I begin to grow
Into a new belief, which saints, nor angels

---

54 *turkey chicken* young turkeys   55 *rails* corn-crakes
56 *affect* please

Could have won me to have faith in.
    Woman. Sir, my lady.   75

Enter LADY.

    Lady. I come to meet you, and languish'd till I
        saw you.
This first kiss is for form; I allow a second
To such a friend.
    Marrall. To such a friend! Heav'n bless me!
    Welborne. I am wholly yours, yet madam, if you
        please
To grace this gentleman with a salute—   80
    Marrall. Salute me at his bidding!
    Welborne. I shall receive it
As a most high favour.
    Lady. Sir, you may command me.
    Welborne. Run backward from a lady? and such a
        lady?
    Marrall. To kiss her foot is to poor me a favour
I am unworthy of— (*Offers to kiss her foot.*)
    Lady. Nay, pray you rise,   85
And since you are so humble, I'll exalt you:
You shall dine with me today, at mine own table.
    Marrall. Your ladyship's table? I am not good
        enough
To sit at your steward's board.
    Lady. You are too modest:
I will not be deni'd.

Enter FURNACE.

    Furnace. Will you still be babbling,   90
Till your meat freeze on the table? the old trick still.
My art ne'er thought on.
    Lady. Your arm, Master Welborne:
Nay keep us company.
    Marrall. I was never so grac'd.
[*Exeunt* WELBORNE, LADY, AMBLE, MARRALL, WOMAN
    [*and* CHAMBERMAID].

80 *salute*— ed. (Q salute.)   81 *bidding!* ed. (Q bidding.)

  Order. So! we have play'd our parts, and are come
   off well.
95 But if I know the mystery, why my lady
  Consented to it, or why Master Welborne
  Desir'd it, may I perish.
   Furnace. Would I had
  The roasting of his heart, that cheated him,
  And forces the poor gentleman to these shifts.
100 By fire (for cooks are Persians, and swear by it),
  Of all the griping, and extorting tyrants
  I ever heard, or read of, I ne'er met
  A match to Sir Giles Overreach.
   Watchall. What will you take
  To tell him so fellow Furnace?
   Furnace. Just as much
  As my throat is worth, for that would be the price
105 on't.
  To have a usurer that starves himself,
  And wears a cloak of one-and-twenty years
  On a suit of fourteen groats, bought of the hangman,
  To grow rich, and then purchase, is too common:
110 But this Sir Giles feeds high, keeps many servants,
  Who must at his command do any outrage;
  Rich in his habit; vast in his expenses;
  Yet he to admiration still increases
  In wealth, and lordships.
   Order. He frights men out of their estates,
  And breaks through all law-nets, made to curb ill
115 men,
  As they were cobwebs. No man dares reprove him.
  Such a spirit to dare, and power to do, were never
  Lodg'd so unluckily.
     Enter AMBLE.
   Amble. Ha, ha; I shall burst.
   Order. Contain thyself man.
   Furnace. Or make us partakers
  Of your sudden mirth.
120 *Amble.* Ha, ha, my lady has got

94 *So! we* ed. (Q So we)
108 *of fourteen groats* worth only a few pence
113 *to admiration* wondrously

Such a guest at her table, this term-driver Marrall,
This snip of an attorney—
   Furnace. What of him man?
   Amble. The knave thinks still he's at the cook's
      shop in Ram-Alley,
Where the clerks divide, and the elder is to choose;
And feeds so slovenly.
   Furnace. Is this all?
   Amble. My lady   125
Drank to him for fashion sake, or to please Master
      Welborne.
As I live he rises, and takes up a dish,
In which there were some remnants of a boil'd
      capon,
And pledges her in whitebroth.
   Furnace. Nay, 'tis like
The rest of his tribe.
   Amble. And when I brought him wine,   130
He leaves his stool, and after a leg or two
Most humbly thanks my worship.
   Order. Rose already.
   Amble. I shall be chid.

        Enter LADY, WELBORNE, MARRALL.

   Furnace. My lady frowns.
   Lady. You wait well.
Let me have no more of this, I observ'd your jeering.
Sirrah, I'll have you know, whom I think worthy   135
To sit at my table, be he ne'er so mean,
When I am present, is not your companion.
   Order. Nay, she'll preserve what's due to her.
   Furnace. This refreshing
Follows your flux of laughter.
   Lady (*to* WELBORNE). You are master
Of your own will. I know so much of manners   140
As not to enquire your purposes, in a word

121 *term-driver* see note on Dramatis Personae
122 *snip* bit (contemptuous)   124 *divide* go shares in a meal
129 *whitebroth* sauce   131 *leg* bow
133 *chid* rebuked
137 *not your companion* not one for you to laugh at
138 *refreshing* cooling dose
139 *flux* discharge

To me you are ever welcome, as to a house
That is your own.
  Welborne. Mark that.
  Marrall. With reverence sir,
And it like your worship.
  Welborne. Trouble yourself no farther,
145 Dear Madam; my heart's full of zeal, and service,
However in my language I am sparing.
Come Master Marrall.
  Marrall. I attend your worship.
       [*Exeunt* WELBORNE, MARRALL.
  Lady. I see in your looks you are sorry, and you
    know me
An easy mistress: be merry; I have forgot all.
150 Order, and Furnace come with me, I must give you
Further directions.
  Order. What you please.
  Furnace. We are ready.   [*Exeunt.*]

Act II, Scene iii

Enter WELBORNE, MARRALL.

  Welborne. I think I am in a good way.
  Marrall. Good, sir? the best way.
The certain best way.
  Welborne. There are casualties
That men are subject to.
  Marrall. You are above 'em,
And as you are already worshipful,
5 I hope ere long you will increase in worship,
And be right worshipful.
  Welborne. Prithee do not flout me.
What I shall be, I shall be. Is't for your ease,
You keep your hat off?
  Marrall. Ease, and it like your worship?
I hope Jack Marrall shall not live so long,
10 To prove himself such an unmannerly beast,
Though it hail hazel nuts, as to be cover'd

1 *Good, sir?* ed. (Q Good sir;) 6 *flout* mock

When your worship's present.

    Welborne (aside). Is not this a true rogue?
That out of mere hope of a future coz'nage
Can turn thus suddenly: 'tis rank already.

    Marrall. I know your worship's wise, and needs no
        counsel: 15
Yet if in my desire to do you service,
I humbly offer my advice, (but still
Under correction) I hope I shall not
Incur your high displeasure.

    Welborne. No; speak freely.

    Marrall. Then in my judgement sir, my simple
        judgement,   20
(Still with your worship's favour) I could wish you
A better habit, for this cannot be
But much distasteful to the noble lady
(I say no more) that loves you, for this morning
To me (and I am but a swine to her)   25
Before th'assurance of her wealth perfum'd you,
You savour'd not of amber.

    Welborne. I do now then?

    Marrall. This your batoon hath got a touch of it.
                          Kisses the end of his cudgel.
Yet if you please for change I have twenty pounds here
Which, out of my true love I presently   30
Lay down at your worship's feet: 'twill serve to buy you
A riding suit.

    Welborne. But where's the horse?

    Marrall. My gelding
Is at your service: nay, you shall ride me
Before your worship shall be put to the trouble
To walk afoot. Alas, when you are lord   35
Of this lady's manor (as I know you will be)
You may with the lease of glebe land, call'd Knave's-
        Acre,
A place I would manure, requite your vassal.

    Welborne. I thank thy love: but must make no use of it.
What's twenty pounds?

13 *coz'nage* cheat   14 *'tis rank* I smell it
25 *to her* compared with her   27 *amber* ambergris
28 *batoon* stick, cudgel   29 *for change* for fresh clothing
37 *glebe land* farm land   38 *manure* farm as tenant

40   *Marrall.* 'Tis all that I can make, sir.
      Welborne. Dost thou think though I want clothes I
            could not have 'em,
      For one word to my lady?
      Marrall. As I know not that!
      Welborne. Come I'll tell thee a secret, and so leave
            thee.
      I'll not give her the advantage, though she be
45   A gallant minded lady, after we are married
      (There being no woman, but is sometimes froward)
      To hit me in the teeth, and say she was forc'd
      To buy my wedding clothes, and took me on
      With a plain riding-suit, and an ambling nag.
50   No, I'll be furnish'd something like myself.
      And so farewell; for thy suit touching Knave's-Acre,
      When it is mine 'tis thine.
      Marrall. I thank your worship.   [*Exit* WELBORNE.
      How was I cozen'd in the calculation
      Of this man's fortune, my master cozen'd too,
55   Whose pupil I am in the art of undoing men,
      For that is our profession; well, well, Master Welborne,
      You are of a sweet nature, and fit again to be cheated:
      Which, if the fates please, when you are possess'd
      Of the land, and lady, you sans question shall be.
      I'll presently think of the means.

            Walk by musing. Enter OVERREACH.

60   *Overreach.* Sirrah, take my horse.
      I'll walk to get me an appetite; 'tis but a mile,
      And exercise will keep me from being pursy.
      Ha! Marrall! is he conjuring? Perhaps
      The knave has wrought the prodigal to do
65   Some outrage on himself, and now he feels
      Compunction in his conscience for't: no matter
      So it be done. Marrall.
      Marrall. Sir.
      Overreach. How succeed we
      In our plot on Welborne?

40 *make* raise in ready money   46 *froward* headstrong, uppish
53 *was I cozen'd* ed. (Q was coozen'd)
s.d. *musing* ed. (Q masing)
67 *done.* Marrall. ed. (Q done, Marrall.)

Marrall. Never better sir.
Overreach. Has he hang'd, or drown'd himself?
Marrall. No sir, he lives.
Lives once more to be made a prey to you,   70
A greater prey than ever.
Overreach. Art thou in thy wits?
If thou art reveal this miracle, and briefly.
Marrall. A lady sir, is fall'n in love with him.
Overreach. With him? what lady?
Marrall. The rich Lady Alworth.
Overreach. Thou dolt; how dar'st thou speak this?
Marrall. I speak truth;   75
And I do so but once a year, unless
It be to you sir, we din'd with her ladyship,
I thank his worship.
Overreach. His worship!
Marrall. As I live sir;
I din'd with him, at the great lady's table,
Simple as I stand here, and saw when she kiss'd him,   80
And would at his request, have kiss'd me too,
But I was not so audacious, as some youths are,
That dare do anything be it ne'er so absurd,
And sad after performance.
Overreach. Why thou rascal,
To tell me these impossibilities: 85
Dine, at her table? and kiss him? or thee?
Impudent varlet. Have not I myself
To whom great countesses' doors have oft flew open,
Ten times attempted, since her husband's death,
In vain to see her, though I came—a suitor;   90
And yet your good solicitor-ship, and rogue Welborne,
Were brought into her presence, feasted with her.
But that I know thee a dog, that cannot blush,
This most incredible lie would call up one
On thy buttermilk cheeks.
Marrall. Shall I not trust my eyes sir?   95
Or taste? I feel her good cheer in my belly.
Overreach. You shall feel me, if you give not over
    sirrah;

83 *That dare* ed. (Q And dare)
91 *rogue Welborne* ed. (Q rogue—Welborne)

Recover your brains again, and be no more gull'd
With a beggar's plot assisted by the aids
100 Of serving-men, and chambermaids (for beyond these
Thou never saw'st a woman), or I'll quit you
From my employments.
    Marrall. Will you credit this yet?
On my confidence of their marriage I offer'd Welborne
(*Aside*) (I would give a crown now, I durst say his
       worship)
My nag, and twenty pounds.
105   *Overreach.* Did you so idiot?   *Strikes him down.*
Was this the way to work him to despair
Or rather to cross me?
    Marrall. Will your worship kill me?
    Overreach. No, no; but drive the lying spirit out
      of thee.
    Marrall. He's gone.
    Overreach. I have done then: now forgetting
110 Your late imaginary feast, and lady,
Know my lord Lovell dines with me tomorrow;
Be careful nought be wanting to receive him,
And bid my daughter's women trim her up,
Though they paint her, so she catch the lord, I'll
      thank 'em;
There's a piece, for my late blows.
115   *Marrall.* I must yet suffer:
(*Aside*) But there may be a time—
    Overreach. Do you grumble?
    Marrall. No sir.   *[Exeunt.]*

Act III, Scene i

Enter LOVELL, ALWORTH, SERVANTS.

Lovell. Walk the horses down the hill: something
    in private,
I must impart to Alworth.   *[Exeunt servi.*
    Alworth. O my lord,
What sacrifice of reverence, duty, watching;
Although I could put off the use of sleep,

105 *idiot?* ed. (Q I doe?)   107 *cross* hinder

And ever wait on your commands to serve 'em;   5
What dangers, though in ne'er so horrid shapes,
Nay death itself, though I should run to meet it,
Can I, and with a thankful willingness suffer;
But still the retribution will fall short
Of your bounties shower'd upon me.
    Lovell. Loving youth;   10
Till what I purpose be put into act,
Do not o'er-prize it; since you have trusted me
With your soul's nearest, nay her dearest secret,
Rest confident 'tis in a cabinet lock'd,
Treachery shall never open. I have found you   15
(For so much to your face I must profess,
Howe'er you guard your modesty with a blush for't)
More zealous in your love, and service to me
Than I have been in my rewards.
    Alworth. Still great ones
Above my merit.
    Lovell. Such your gratitude calls 'em: 20
Nor am I of that harsh, and rugged temper
As some great men are tax'd with, who imagine
They part from the respect due to their honours,
If they use not all such as follow 'em,
Without distinction of their births, like slaves.   25
I am not so condition'd: I can make
A fitting difference between my foot-boy,
And a gentleman, by want compell'd to serve me.
    Alworth. 'Tis thankfully acknowledg'd: you have
      been
More like a father to me than a master.   30
Pray you pardon the comparison.
    Lovell. I allow it;
And to give you assurance I am pleas'd in't,
My carriage and demeanour to your mistress
Fair Margaret, shall truly witness for me
I can command my passions.
    Alworth. 'Tis a conquest   35
Few lords can boast of when they are tempted. Oh!

5 *to serve* ed. (Q serve)   21 *rugged* ed. (Q rugg'd)
26 *so conditioned* of such character   31 *allow* approve
33 *carriage and demeanour* behaviour

Lovell. Why do you sigh? Can you be doubtful of
    me?
By that fair name, I in the wars have purchas'd,
And all my actions hitherto untainted,
40   I will not be more true to mine own honour,
Than to my Alworth.
    Alworth. As you are the brave Lord Lovell,
Your bare word only given, is an assurance
Of more validity, and weight to me
Than all the oaths bound up with imprecations,
Which when they would deceive, most courtiers
45   practise:
Yet being a man (for sure to style you more
Would relish of gross flattery) I am forc'd,
Against my confidence of your worth, and virtues,
To doubt, nay more to fear.
    Lovell. So young, and jealous?
50   *Alworth.* Were you to encounter with a single foe,
The victory were certain: but to stand
The charge of two such potent enemies,
At once assaulting you, as wealth and beauty,
And those too seconded with power, is odds
Too great for Hercules.
55   *Lovell.* Speak your doubts, and fears,
Since you will nourish 'em, in plainer language,
That I may understand 'em.
    Alworth. What's your will,
Though I lend arms against myself (provided
They may advantage you), must be obeyed.
60   My much lov'd lord, were Margaret only fair,
The cannon of her more than earthly form,
Though mounted high, commanding all beneath it,
And ramm'd with bullets of her sparkling eyes,
Of all the bulwarks that defend your senses
65   Could batter none, but that which guards your sight.
But when the well tun'd accents of her tongue
Make music to you, and with numerous sounds
Assault your hearing (such as if Ulysses
Now liv'd again, howe'er he stood the Sirens,
70   Could not resist) the combat must grow doubtful,

65 *none* ed. (Q *more*)   67 *numerous* in musical cadence

Between your reason, and rebellious passions.
Add this too; when you feel her touch, and breath,
Like a soft western wind, when it glides o'er
Arabia, creating gums, and spices:
And in the van, the nectar of her lips   75
Which you must taste, bring the battalia on,
Well arm'd, and strongly lin'd with her discourse,
And knowing manners, to give entertainment,
Hippolytus himself would leave Diana,
To follow such a Venus.
    Lovell. Love hath made you   80
Poetical, Alworth.
    Alworth. Grant all these beat off,
Which if it be in man to do, you'll do it;
Mammon in Sir Giles Overreach steps in
With heaps of ill got gold, and so much land,
To make her more remarkable, as would tire   85
A falcon's wings in one day to fly over.
O my good lord, these powerful aids, which would
Make a misshapen negro beautiful
(Yet are but ornaments to give her lustre,
That in her self is all perfection), must   90
Prevail for her. I here release your trust.
'Tis happiness, enough, for me to serve you,
And sometimes with chaste eyes to look upon her.
    Lovell. Why, shall I swear?
    Alworth. O by no means my lord;
And wrong not so your judgement to the world   95
As from your fond indulgence to a boy,
Your page, your servant, to refuse a blessing
Divers great men are rivals for.
    Lovell. Suspend
Your judgement till the trial. How far is it
T'Overreach' house?
    Alworth. At the most some half hour's riding;   100
You'll soon be there.
    Lovell. And you the sooner freed
From your jealous fears.
    Alworth. O that I durst but hope it.   [*Exeunt.*

75 *in the van* in the front rank
76 *battalia* main body of troops   77 *lin'd* reinforced

Act III, Scene ii

Enter OVERREACH, GREEDY, MARRALL.

Overreach. Spare for no cost, let my dressers
        crack with the weight
Of curious viands.
        Greedy. Store indeed's no sore, sir.
        Overreach. That proverb fits your stomach Master
        Greedy.
And let no plate be seen, but what's pure gold,
5 Or such whose workmanship exceeds the matter
That it is made of; let my choicest linen
Perfume the room, and when we wash, the water
With precious powders mix'd, so please my lord,
That he may with envy wish to bathe so ever.
        Marrall. 'Twill be very chargeable.
10   *Overreach.* Avaunt you drudge:
Now all my labour'd ends are at the stake,
Is't a time to think of thrift? Call in my daughter;
                        [*Exit* MARRALL.]
And Master Justice, since you love choice dishes,
And plenty of 'em—
        Greedy. As I do indeed sir,
15 Almost as much as to give thanks for 'em.
        Overreach. I do confer that providence, with my
        power
Of absolute command to have abundance,
To your best care.
        Greedy. I'll punctually discharge it
And give the best directions. Now am I
20 In mine own conceit a monarch, at the least
Arch-president of the boil'd, the roast, the bak'd,
For which I will eat often, and give thanks,
When my belly's brac'd up like a drum, and that's
            pure justice.   [*Exit* GREEDY.

2 *Store indeed's no sore* One cannot have too much of a good thing
10 *chargeable* expensive   14 *of 'em—* ed. (Q of 'em.)
16 *providence* purveyorship   20 *conceit* imagination
23 *brac'd up* pulled tight

Overreach. It must be so: should the foolish girl
    prove modest,
She may spoil all, she had it not from me,   25
But from her mother, I was ever forward,
As she must be, and therefore I'll prepare her.

[*Enter*] MARGARET.

Alone, and let your women wait without.
    Margaret. Your pleasure sir?
    Overreach. Ha, this is a neat dressing!
These orient pearls, and diamonds well plac'd too!   30
The gown affects me not, it should have been
Embroider'd o'er, and o'er with flowers of gold,
But these rich jewels, and quaint fashion help it.
And how below? since oft the wanton eye
The face observ'd, descends unto the foot;   35
Which being well proportion'd, as yours is,
Invites as much as perfect white, and red,
Though without art. How like you your new woman
The Lady Downefalne?
    Margaret. Well for a companion;
Not as a servant.
    Overreach. Is she humble Meg?   40
And careful too; her ladyship forgotten?
    Margaret. I pity her fortune.
    Overreach. Pity her? Trample on her.
I took her up in an old tamin gown,
(Even starv'd for want of twopenny chop) to serve
    thee:
And if I understand, she but repines   45
To do thee any duty, though ne'er so servile,
I'll pack her to her knight, where I have lodg'd him,
Into the Counter, and there let 'em howl together.
    Margaret. You know your own ways, but for me I
    blush
When I command her, that was once attended   50

24 *It must* ed. (Q I must)
31 *affects* pleases   37 *invites* entices
41 *careful* industrious   43 *tamin* thin woollen stuff
44 *twopenny chop* ed. (Q two penny chopps) a thin stew
48 *the Counter* a debtors' prison

With persons, not inferior to my self
In birth.
    Overreach. In birth? Why, art thou not my daughter?
The blest child of my industry, and wealth?
Why foolish girl, was't not to make thee great,
55 That I have ran, and still pursue those ways
That hale down curses on me, which I mind not.
Part with these humble thoughts, and apt thy self
To the noble state I labour to advance thee,
Or by my hopes to see thee honourable,
60 I will adopt a stranger to my heir,
And throw thee from my care, do not provoke me.
    Margaret. I will not sir; mould me which way you
      please.

Enter GREEDY.

    Overreach. How, interrupted?
    Greedy. 'Tis matter of importance.
The cook sir is self-will'd and will not learn
From my experience, there's a fawn brought in
65   sir,
And for my life I cannot make him roast it,
With a Norfolk dumpling in the belly of it.
And sir, we wisemen know, without the dumpling
'Tis not worth threepence.
    Overreach. Would it were whole in thy belly
70 To stuff it out; cook it any way, prithee leave me.
    Greedy. Without order for the dumpling?
    Overreach. Let it be dumpl'd
Which way thou wilt, or tell him I will scald him
In his own cauldron.
    Greedy. I had lost my stomach,
Had I lost my mistress dumpling, I'll give thanks for.
                   [*Exit* GREEDY.
    Overreach. But to our business Meg, you have heard
75   who dines here?
    Margaret. I have sir.
    Overreach. 'Tis an honourable man,
A lord, Meg, and commands a regiment
Of soldiers, and what's rare is one himself;
A bold, and understanding one; and to be

A lord, and a good leader in one volume,   80
Is granted unto few, but such as rise up
The kingdom's glory.   *Enter* GREEDY.
   Greedy. I'll resign my office,
If I be not better obey'd.
   Overreach. 'Slight, art thou frantic?
   Greedy. Frantic, 'twould make me a frantic, and
      stark-mad,
Were I not a justice of peace, and *coram* too,   85
Which this rebellious cook cares not a straw for.
There are a dozen of woodcocks.
   Overreach. Make thyself
Thirteen, the baker's dozen.
   Greedy. I am contented
So they may be dress'd to my mind, he has found out
A new device for sauce, and will not dish 'em   90
With toasts, and butter, my father was a tailor,
And my name though a justice, Greedy Woodcock,
And ere I'll see my lineage so abus'd,
I'll give up my commission.
   Overreach. Cook, rogue obey him.
I have given the word, pray you now remove yourself,   95
To a collar of brawn, and trouble me no farther.
   Greedy. I will, and meditate what to eat at dinner.
                   [*Exit* GREEDY.
   Overreach. And as I said Meg, when this gull
      disturb'd us;
This honourable lord, this colonel
I would have thy husband.
   Margaret. There's too much disparity   100
Between his quality, and mine to hope it.
   Overreach. I more than hope't, and doubt not to
      effect it.
Be thou no enemy to thyself, my wealth
Shall weigh his titles down, and make you equals.
Now for the means to assure him thine; observe me;   105
Remember he's a courtier, and a soldier,
And not to be trifl'd with, and therefore when
He comes to woo you, see you, do not coy it.

80 *in one volume* both at once   84 *a frantic* a lunatic
85 *coram* for *quorum*, cf. I.i, 34   101 *quality* rank

This mincing modesty hath spoil'd many a match
110 By a first refusal, in vain after hop'd for.
    Margaret. You'll have me sir, preserve the distance,
        that
Confines a virgin?
    Overreach. Virgin me no virgins.
I must have you lose that name, or you lose me;
I will have you private, start not, I say private.
115 If thou art my true daughter, not a bastard,
Thou wilt venture alone with one man, though he
        came
Like Jupiter to Semele, and come off too.
And therefore when he kisses you, kiss close.
    Margaret. I have heard this is the strumpet's
        fashion sir,
Which I must never learn.
120   *Overreach.* Learn anything,
And from any creature that may make thee great;
From the devil himself.
    Margaret. This is but devilish doctrine.
    Overreach. Or if his blood grow hot, suppose he
       offer
Beyond this, do not you stay till it cool,
125 But meet his ardour, if a couch be near,
Sit down on't, and invite him.
    Margaret. In your house?
Your own house sir, for heav'n's sake, what are you
       then?
Or what shall I be sir?
    Overreach. Stand not on form,
Words are no substances.
    Margaret. Though you could dispense
130 With your own honour; cast aside religion,
The hopes of heaven, or fear of hell, excuse me,
In worldly policy, this is not the way
To make me his wife, his whore I grant it may do.
My maiden honour so soon yielded up,
135 Nay prostituted, cannot but assure him
I that am light to him will not hold weight

114 *private* intimate, familiar   123 *offer* attempt
132 *policy* prudence, cunning
136 *light* unchaste (with a play on 'weight')

When his, tempted by others: so in judgement
When to his lust I have given up my honour
He must, and will forsake me.
    Overreach. How? forsake thee?
Do I wear a sword for fashion? or is this arm   140
Shrunk up? or wither'd? does there live a man
Of that large list I have encounter'd with,
Can truly say I e'er gave inch of ground,
Not purchas'd with his blood, that did oppose me?
Forsake thee when the thing is done? he dares not.   145
Give me but proof, he has enjoy'd thy person,
Though all his captains, echoes to his will,
Stood arm'd by his side to justify the wrong,
And he himself in the head of his bold troop,
Spite of his lordship, and his colonelship,   150
Or the judge's favour, I will make him render
A bloody and a strict accompt, and force him
By marrying thee, to cure thy wounded honour;
I have said it.

Enter MARRALL.

    Marrall. Sir, the man of honour's come
Newly alighted.
    Overreach. In; without reply;   155
And do as I command, or thou art lost.
                                    [Exit MARGARET.
Is the loud music I have order for
Ready to receive him?
    Marrall. 'Tis sir.
    Overreach. Let 'em sound
A princely welcome. *[Exit* MARRALL.] Roughness
        awhile leave me,
For fawning now, a stranger to my nature   160
Must make way for me.

Loud music. Enter LOVELL, GREEDY, ALWORTH,
MARRALL.

    Lovell. Sir, you meet your trouble.
    Overreach. What you are pleas'd to style so is an
honour

137 *When his, tempted* ed. (Q When he is tempted)

Above my worth, and fortunes.

Alworth. Strange, so humble.

Overreach. A justice of peace my lord.

Presents GREEDY to him.

Lovell. Your hand good sir.

165   *Greedy.* This is a lord, and some think this a favour;
But I had rather have my hand in my dumpling.

Overreach. Room for my lord.

Lovell. I miss sir your fair daughter,
To crown my welcome.

Overreach. May it please my lord
To taste a glass of Greek wine first, and suddenly
She shall attend my lord.

170   *Lovell.* You'll be obey'd sir.

[Exeunt omnes praeter OVERREACH.

Overreach. 'Tis to my wish; as soon as come ask for
   her!

Why, Meg? Meg Overreach. [*Enter* MARGARET.] How!
   tears in your eyes!

Ha! dry 'em quickly, or I'll dig 'em out.

Is this a time to whimper? meet that greatness

175   That flies into thy bosom, think what 'tis
For me to say, My honourable daughter.
And thou, when I stand bare, to say Put on,
Or Father you forget yourself, no more,
But be instructed, or expect—he comes.

Enter LOVELL, GREEDY, ALWORTH, MARRALL.
They salute.

A black-brow'd girl my lord.

180   *Lovell.* As I live a rare one.

Alworth. He's took already: I am lost.

Overreach. That kiss
Came twanging off, I like it, quit the room:

[The rest off.

A little bashful my good lord, but you
I hope will teach her boldness.

Lovell. I am happy
In such a scholar: but—

s.d. *praeter* ed. (Q preter) except 177 *bare* with hat in hand
179 *expect*—ed. (Q expect.)   185 *but*— ed. (Q but.)

Overreach. I am past learning.   185
And therefore leave you to yourselves: (*to his daughter*)
       remember—   [*Exit* OVERREACH.
  Lovell. You see fair lady, your father is solicitous
To have you change the barren name of virgin
Into a hopeful wife.
  Margaret. His haste my lord,
Holds no power o'er my will.
  Lovell. But o'er your duty.   190
  Margaret. Which forc'd too much may break.
  Lovell. Bend rather sweetest:
Think of your years.
  Margaret. Too few to match with yours:
And choicest fruits too soon pluck'd, rot, and wither.
  Lovell. Do you think I am old?
  Margaret. I am sure I am too young.
  Lovell. I can advance you.
  Margaret. To a hill of sorrow,   195
Where every hour I may expect to fall,
But never hope firm footing. You are noble,
I of a low descent, however rich;
And tissues match'd with scarlet suit but ill.
O my good lord I could say more, but that   200
I dare not trust these walls.
  Lovell. Pray you trust my ear then.

       Enter OVERREACH, *listening.*

  Overreach. Close at it! whispering! this is excellent!
And by their postures, a consent on both parts.

          Enter GREEDY.

  Greedy. Sir Giles, Sir Giles.
  Overreach. The great fiend stop that clapper.
  Greedy. It must ring out sir, when my belly rings
      noon.   205
The bak'd meats are run out, the roast turn'd powder.
  Overreach. I shall powder you.

189 *His haste* ed. (Q He hast)
206 *bak'd* ed. (Q back'd)
206 *run out* escaped through the crust
206 *turn'd powder* cooked dry

Greedy. Beat me to dust I care not.
In such a cause as this, I'll die a martyr.
   Overreach. Marry and shall: you barathrum of the
      shambles.   *Strikes him.*
   Greedy. How! strike a justice of peace? 'tis petty
210   treason,
Edwardi quinto, but that you are my friend
I could commit you without bail or main-prise.
   Overreach. Leave your bawling sir, or I shall commit
      you,
Where you shall not dine today, disturb my lord,
When he is in discourse?
215   *Greedy.* Is't a time to talk
When we should be munching?
   Lovell. Ha! I heard some noise.
   Overreach. Mum, villain, vanish: shall we break a
      bargain
Almost made up?   *[Thrust* GREEDY *off.*
   Lovell. Lady I understand you;
And rest most happy in your choice, believe it;
220 I'll be a careful pilot to direct
Your yet uncertain bark to a port of safety.
   Margaret. So shall your honour save two lives, and
      bind us
Your slaves for ever.
   Lovell. I am in the act rewarded,
Since it is good, howe'er you must put on
225 An amorous carriage towards me, to delude
Your subtle father.
   Margaret. I am prone to that.
   Lovell. Now break we off our conference. Sir Giles.
Where is Sir Giles?

     Enter OVERREACH, *and the rest.*

   Overreach. My noble lord; and how
Does your lordship find her?
   Lovell. Apt Sir Giles, and coming,
And I like her the better.
230   *Overreach.* So do I too.

211 *Edwardi quinto* cf. I.iii. 30 note   212 *main-prise* surety
225 *An* ed. (Q And)   229 *coming* not bashful

Lovell. Yet should we take forts at the first assault
'Twere poor in the defendant; I must confirm her
With a love letter or two, which I must have
Deliver'd by my page, and you give way to't.

Overreach. With all my soul, a towardly gentleman. 235
Your hand good Master Alworth, know my house
Is ever open to you.

Alworth (aside). 'Twas shut till now.

Overreach. Well done, well done, my honourable
      daughter:
Th'art so already: know this gentle youth,
And cherish him my honourable daughter. 240

Margaret. I shall with my best care.

                    Noise within as of a coach.

Overreach. A coach.

Greedy. More stops
Before we go to dinner! O my guts!

         Enter LADY, *and* WELBORNE.

Lady. If I find welcome
You share in it; if not I'll back again,
Now I know your ends, for I come arm'd for all 245
Can be objected.

Lovell. How! the Lady Alworth!

Overreach. And thus attended!

    LOVELL *salutes the* LADY, *the* LADY *salutes*
    MARGARET.

Marrall. No, I am a dolt;
The spirit of lies had enter'd me.

Overreach. Peace patch,
'Tis more than wonder! an astonishment
That does possess me wholly!

Lovell. Noble lady, 250
This is a favour to prevent my visit,
The service of my life can never equal.

Lady. My lord, I laid wait for you, and much hop'd
You would have made my poor house your first inn:
And therefore doubting that you might forget me, 255
Or too long dwell here having such ample cause

234 *and* if   235 *towardly* promising
248 *patch* fool   251 *prevent* forestall, anticipate

In this unequall'd beauty for your stay;
And fearing to trust any but myself
With the relation of my service to you,
260 I borrow'd so much from my long restraint,
And took the air in person to invite you.
    Lovell. Your bounties are so great they rob me,
            madam,
Of words to give you thanks.
    Lady. Good Sir Giles Overreach. (*Salutes him.*)
How dost thou Marrall? lik'd you my meat so ill,
265 You'll dine no more with me?
    Greedy. I will when you please
And it like your ladyship.
    Lady. When you please Master Greedy.
If meat can do it, you shall be satisfied.
And now my lord, pray take into your knowledge
This gentleman, howe'er his outside's coarse,
            (*presents* WELBORNE)
270 His inward linings are as fine, and fair,
As any man's: wonder not I speak at large:
And howsoe'er his humour carries him
To be thus accoutred; or what taint soever
For his wild life hath stuck upon his fame,
275 He may ere long, with boldness, rank himself
With some that have contemn'd him. Sir Giles
            Overreach,
If I am welcome, bid him so.
    Overreach. My nephew.
He has been too long a stranger: faith you have:
Pray let it be mended.
            LOVELL *conferring with* WELBORNE.
    Marrall. Why sir, what do you mean?
280 This is rogue Welborne, monster, prodigy,
That should hang, or drown himself, no man of
            worship,
Much less your nephew.
    Overreach. Well sirrah, we shall reckon
For this hereafter.
    Marrall. I'll not lose my jeer
Though I be beaten dead for't.

271 *speak at large* praise him freely   272 *humour* whim

Welborne. Let my silence plead
In my excuse my lord till better leisure   285
Offer itself to hear a full relation
Of my poor fortunes.
    Lovell. I would hear, and help 'em.
    Overreach. Your dinner waits you.
    Lovell. Pray you lead, we follow.
    Lady. Nay you are my guest, come dear Master
        Welborne.   [*Exeunt: manet* GREEDY.
    Greedy. Dear Master Welborne! So she said;
        heav'n! heav'n!   290
If my belly would give me leave I could ruminate
All day on this: I have granted twenty warrants,
To have him committed, from all prisons in the shire,
To Nottingham gaol; and now dear Master
        Welborne!
And my good nephew, but I play the fool   295
To stand here prating, and forget my dinner.

Enter MARRALL.

Are they set Marrall?
    Marrall. Long since, pray you a word sir.
    Greedy. No wording now.
    Marrall. In troth, I must; my master
Knowing you are his good friend, makes bold with
        you,
And does entreat you, more guests being come in,   300
Than he expected, especially his nephew,
The table being full too, you would excuse him
And sup with him on the cold meat.
    Greedy. How! no dinner
After all my care?
    Marrall. 'Tis but a penance for
A meal; besides, you broke your fast.
    Greedy. That was   305
But a bit to stay my stomach: a man in commission
Give place to a tatterdemalion?
    Marrall. No bug words sir.

s.d. *manet* remains   297 *set* seated at table
302 *excuse him* forgive his not inviting you
307 *tatterdemalion* beggarly knave; *bug words* threats

Should his worship hear you—
Greedy. Lose my dumpling too?
And butter'd toasts, and woodcocks?
Marrall. Come, have patience.
310 If you will dispense a little with your worship,
And sit with the waiting women, you have dumpling,
Woodcock and butter'd toasts too.
Greedy. This revives me.
I will gorge there sufficiently.
Marrall. This is the way sir.   [*Exeunt*.

Act III, Scene iii

Enter OVERREACH *as from dinner*.

Overreach. She's caught! O women! she neglects
    my lord,
And all her compliments appli'd to Welborne!
The garments of her widowhood laid by,
She now appears as glorious as the spring.
5 Her eyes fix'd on him, in the wine she drinks,
He being her pledge, she sends him burning kisses,
And sits on thorns, till she be private with him.
She leaves my meat to feed upon his looks;
And if in our discourse he be but nam'd
10 From her a deep sigh follows, but why grieve I
At this? it makes for me, if she prove his,
All that is hers is mine, as I will work him.

Enter MARRALL.

Marrall. Sir the whole board is troubled at your
    rising.
Overreach. No matter, I'll excuse it, prithee
    Marrall,
15 Watch an occasion to invite my nephew
To speak with me in private.
Marrall. Who? the rogue,

308 *hear you* — ed. (Q heare you?)
310 *worship* dignity
  2 *compliments appli'd* courtesies [are] directed

The lady scorn'd to look on?
   Overreach. You are a wag.

Enter LADY *and* WELBORNE.

   Marrall. See sir she's come, and cannot be without
      him.
   Lady. With your favour sir, after a plenteous
      dinner,
I shall make bold to walk a turn, or two   20
In your rare garden.
   Overreach. There's an arbour too
If your ladyship please to use it.
   Lady. Come Master Welborne.
[*Exeunt* LADY *and* WELBORNE.
   Overreach. Grosser, and grosser, now I believe the
      poet
Feign'd not but was historical, when he wrote
Pasiphae was enamour'd of a bull,   25
This lady's lust's more monstrous. My good lord,

(*Enter* LOVELL, MARGARET *and the rest.*)

Excuse my manners.
   Lovell. There needs none Sir Giles,
I may ere long say Father, when it pleases
My dearest mistress to give warrant to it.
   Overreach. She shall seal to it my lord, and make
      me happy.   30
   Margaret. My lady is return'd.

Enter WELBORNE *and the* LADY.

   Lady. Provide my coach,
I'll instantly away: my thanks Sir Giles
For my entertainment.
   Overreach. 'Tis your nobleness
To think it such.
   Lady. I must do you a further wrong
In taking away your honourable guest.   35
   Lovell. I wait on you madam, farewell good Sir
      Giles.

27 *excuse my manners* in leaving the table first

Lady. Good mistress Margaret: nay come Master
    Welborne,
I must not leave you behind, in sooth I must not.
Overreach. Rob me not madam, of all joys at once;
40 Let my nephew stay behind: he shall have my coach,
And (after some small conference between us)
Soon overtake your ladyship.
    Lady. Stay not long sir.
    Lovell. This parting kiss: you shall every day hear
    from me
By my faithful page.
    Alworth. 'Tis a service I am proud of.
        [Exeunt LOVELL, LADY, ALWORTH, MARGARET,
        MARRALL.
    Overreach. Daughter to your chamber. You may
45   wonder nephew,
After so long an enmity between us
I should desire your friendship?
    Welborne. So I do sir,
'Tis strange to me.
    Overreach. But I'll make it no wonder,
And what is more unfold my nature to you.
50 We worldly men, when we see friends, and kinsmen,
Past hope sunk in their fortunes, lend no hand
To lift 'em up, but rather set our feet
Upon their heads, to press 'em to the bottom,
As I must yield, with you I practis'd it.
55 But now I see you in a way to rise,
I can and will assist you; this rich lady
(And I am glad of't) is enamour'd of you;
'Tis too apparent nephew.
    Welborne. No such thing:
Compassion rather sir.
    Overreach. Well in a word,
60 Because your stay is short, I'll have you seen
No more in this base shape; nor shall she say
She married you like a beggar, or in debt.
    Welborne (aside). He'll run into the noose, and save
    my labour.

47 Welborne. *So I do sir* ed. (Q Well: so I doe Sir)
54 *yield* concede   61 *shape* costume

Overreach. You have a trunk of rich clothes, not
    far hence
In pawn, I will redeem 'em, and that no clamour   65
May taint your credit for your petty debts,
You shall have a thousand pounds to cut 'em off,
And go a freeman to the wealthy lady.
    Welborne. This done sir out of love, and no ends
    else—
    Overreach. As it is nephew.
    Welborne. Binds me still your servant.   70
    Overreach. No compliments; you are stay'd for;
    ere y'ave supp'd
You shall hear from me, my coach knaves for my
    nephew:
Tomorrow I will visit you.
    Welborne. Here's an uncle
In a man's extremes! how much they do belie you
That say you are hard-hearted.
    Overreach. My deeds nephew   75
Shall speak my love, what men report, I weigh not.
            [Exeunt: finis Actus tertii.

Act IV, Scene i

Enter LOVELL, ALWORTH.

Lovell. 'Tis well: give me my cloak: I now
    discharge you
From further service. Mind your own affairs,
I hope they will prove successful.
    Alworth. What is blest
With your good wish my lord, cannot but prosper.
Let after-times report, and to your honour,   5
How much I stand engag'd, for I want language
To speak my debt: yet if a tear, or two
Of joy for your much goodness, can supply
My tongue's defects, I could—
    Lovell. Nay, do not melt:

69 *no ends else—* ed. (Q no ends else.)   70 *me* ed. (Q my)
  9 *I could—* ed. (Q I could.)

10   This ceremonial thanks to me's superfluous.
         Overreach (*within*). Is my lord stirring?
         Lovell. 'Tis he, oh here's your letter: let him in.

                Enter OVERREACH, GREEDY, MARRALL.

         Overreach. A good day to my lord.
         Lovell. You are an early riser,
      Sir Giles.
         Overreach. And reason, to attend your lordship.
15   *Lovell.* And you too Master Greedy, up so soon?
         Greedy. In troth my lord after the sun is up
      I cannot sleep, for I have a foolish stomach
      That croaks for breakfast. With your lordship's
              favour;
      I have a serious question to demand
      Of my worthy friend Sir Giles.
20   *Lovell.* Pray you use your pleasure.
         Greedy. How far Sir Giles, and pray you answer me
      Upon your credit, hold you it to be
      From your manor house, to this of my Lady Alworth?
         Overreach. Why some four mile.
         Greedy. How! four mile? good Sir Giles.
25   Upon your reputation think better;
      For if you do abate but one half quarter
      Of five you do yourself the greatest wrong
      That can be in the world: for four miles' riding
      Could not have rais'd so huge an appetite
      As I feel gnawing on me.
30   *Marrall.* Whether you ride,
      Or go afoot, you are that way still provided
      And it please your worship.
         Overreach. How now sirrah? prating
      Before my lord: no difference? go to my nephew;
      See all his debts discharg'd, and help his worship
      To fit on his rich suit.
35   *Marrall.* I may fit you too;
      Toss'd like a dog still.   [*Exit* MARRALL.

      ---

      30 *Whether* ed. (Q Whither)
      31, 36 *still* always
      33 *difference* distinction of persons
      35 *fit you* settle you, pay you out

    Lovell. I have writ this morning
A few lines to my mistress your fair daughter.
    Overreach. 'Twill fire her, for she's wholly yours
        already:
Sweet Master Alworth, take my ring, 'twill carry you
To her presence I dare warrant you, and there plead   40
For my good lord, if you shall find occasion.
That done, pray ride to Nottingham, get a licence,
Still by this token, I'll have it dispatch'd,
And suddenly my lord, that I may say
My honourable, nay, right honourable daughter.   45
    Greedy. Take my advice young gentleman: get
        your breakfast.
'Tis unwholesome to ride fasting, I'll eat with you,
And eat to purpose.
    Overreach. Some fury's in that gut:
Hungry again! did you not devour this morning,
A shield of brawn, and a barrel of Colchester
        oysters?   50
    Greedy. Why that was sir, only to scour my
        stomach,
A kind of a preparative. Come gentleman,
I will not have you feed like the hangman of Flushing
Alone, while I am here.
    Lovell. Haste your return.
    Alworth. I will not fail my lord.
    Greedy. Nor I to line   55
My Christmas coffer.
              [*Exeunt* GREEDY *and* ALWORTH.
    Overreach. To my wish, we are private.
I come not to make offer with my daughter
A certain portion, that were poor, and trivial:
In one word I pronounce all that is mine,
In lands, or leases, ready coin, or goods,   60
With her, my lord, comes to you, nor shall you have

48 *fury's* ed. (Q Furies)
50 *shield of brawn* brawn cooked in pigskin, the whole dish
51 *scour my stomach* serve as an appetizer
53 *hangman of Flushing* (Q Vllushing) with whom no one would
    sit at meat
56 *Christmas coffer* stomach, container for Christmas fare
58 *certain portion* stated dowry

One motive to induce you to believe
I live too long, since every year I'll add
Something unto the heap, which shall be yours too.
    Lovell. You are a right kind father.
65   *Overreach.* You shall have reason
To think me such; how do you like this seat?
It is well wooded, and well water'd, the acres
Fertile, and rich; would it not serve for change
To entertain your friends in a summer progress?
What thinks my noble lord?
70   *Lovell.* 'Tis a wholesome air,
And well built pile, and she that's mistress of it
Worthy the large revenue.
    Overreach. She the mistress?
It may be so for a time: but let my lord
Say only that he likes it, and would have it,
I say ere long 'tis his.
75   *Lovell.* Impossible.
    Overreach. You do conclude too fast, not knowing
        me;
Nor the engines that I work by, 'tis not alone
The Lady Alworth's lands, for those, once
        Welborne's
(As by her dotage on him, I know they will be),
80 Shall soon be mine, but point out any man's
In all the shire, and say they lie convenient,
And useful for your lordship, and once more
I say aloud, they are yours.
    Lovell. I dare not own
What's by unjust, and cruel means extorted.
85 My fame, and credit are more dear to me,
Than so to expose 'em to be censur'd by
The public voice.
    Overreach. You run my lord no hazard.
Your reputation shall stand as fair
In all good men's opinions as now:
90 Nor can my actions, though condemn'd for ill,
Cast any foul aspersion upon yours;
For though I do contemn report myself,
As a mere sound, I still will be so tender

69 *progress* country tour   77 *engines* contrivances

Of what concerns you in all points of honour,
That the immaculate whiteness of your fame,   95
Nor your unquestion'd integrity
Shall e'er be sullied with one taint, or spot
That may take from your innocence, and candour.
All my ambition is to have my daughter
Right honourable, which my lord can make her.   100
And might I live to dance upon my knee
A young Lord Lovell, borne by her unto you,
I write *nil ultra* to my proudest hopes.
As for possessions, and annual rents
Equivalent to maintain you in the port   105
Your noble birth, and present state requires,
I do remove that burden from your shoulders,
And take it on mine own: for though I ruin
The country to supply your riotous waste,
The scourge of prodigals, want, shall never find you.   110
　　Lovell. Are you not frighted with the imprecations,
And curses, of whole families made wretched
By your sinister practices?
　　Overreach. Yes, as rocks are
When foamy billows split themselves against
Their flinty ribs; or as the moon is mov'd,   115
When wolves with hunger pin'd, howl at her
　　　　brightness.
I am of a solid temper, and like these
Steer on a constant course: with mine own sword
If call'd into the field, I can make that right,
Which fearful enemies murmur'd at as wrong.   120
Now, for these other piddling complaints
Breath'd out in bitterness, as when they call me
Extortioner, tyrant, cormorant, or intruder
On my poor neighbour's right, or grand encloser
Of what was common, to my private use;   125
Nay, when my ears are pierc'd with widows' cries,
And undone orphans wash with tears my threshold;
I only think what 'tis to have my daughter

103 *nil ultra* 'nothing beyond this'
105 *equivalent* of sufficient value; *port* station
113 *sinister* left-handed, dishonest   121 *piddling* trifling
126 *ears* ed. (Q cares)

Right honourable; and 'tis a powerful charm
130 Makes me insensible of remorse, or pity,
Or the least sting of conscience.
   Lovell. I admire
The toughness of your nature.
   Overreach. 'Tis for you
My lord, and for my daughter, I am marble.
Nay, more, if you will have my character
135 In little, I enjoy more true delight
In my arrival to my wealth, these dark
And crooked ways, than you shall e'er take pleasure
In spending what my industry hath compass'd.
My haste commands me hence, in one word therefore
Is it a match?
140   *Lovell.* I hope that is past doubt now.
   Overreach. Then rest secure, not the hate of all
      mankind here,
Nor fear of what can fall on me hereafter,
Shall make me study aught but your advancement,
One story higher. An earl! if gold can do it.
145 Dispute not my religion, nor my faith,
Though I am borne thus headlong by my will,
You may make choice of what belief you please,
To me they are equal, so my lord good morrow. [*Exit.*
   Lovell. He's gone, I wonder how the earth can bear
150 Such a portent! I, that have liv'd a soldier,
And stood the enemy's violent charge undaunted
To hear this blasphemous beast am bath'd all over
In a cold sweat: yet like a mountain he,
Confirm'd in atheistical assertions,
155 Is no more shaken, than Olympus is
When angry Boreas loads his double head
With sudden drifts of snow.

       Enter AMBLE, LADY, WOMAN.

   Lady. Save you my lord.
Disturb I not your privacy?
   Lovell. No good madam;

131 *admire* wonder at   135 *more* ed. (Q more more)
145 *dispute* object   150 *portent* prodigy of evil
151 *enemy's* ed. (Q enemies)   152 *am* ed. (Q a'm)

For your own sake I am glad you came no sooner.
Since this bold, bad man, Sir Giles Overreach   160
Made such a plain discovery of himself,
And read this morning such a devilish matins,
That I should think it a sin next to his,
But to repeat it.
    Lady. I ne'er press'd my lord
On others' privacies, yet against my will,   165
Walking, for health sake, in the gallery
Adjoining to your lodgings, I was made
(So vehement, and loud he was) partaker
Of his tempting offers.
    Lovell. Please you to command
Your servants hence, and I shall gladly hear   170
Your wiser counsel.
    Lady. 'Tis my lord a woman's,
But true, and hearty; wait in the next room,
But be within call: yet not so near to force me
To whisper my intents.
    Amble. We are taught better
By you good madam.
    Woman. And well know our distance.   175
    Lady. Do so, and talk not, 'twill become your
        breeding.   [*Exeunt* AMBLE *and* WOMAN.
Now my good lord; if I may use my freedom,
As to an honour'd friend—
    Lovell. You lessen else
Your favour to me.
    Lady. I dare then say thus;
As you are noble (howe'er common men   180
Make sordid wealth the object, and sole end
Of their industrious aims) 'twill not agree
With those of eminent blood (who are engag'd
More to prefer their honours, than to increase
The state left to 'em, by their ancestors)   185
To study large additions to their fortunes
And quite neglect their births: though I must grant
Riches well got to be a useful servant,
But a bad master.

169 Lovell ed. (Q Lad[y].)   178 *friend—* ed. (Q friend?)
184 *prefer* advance   185 *state* estate

Lovell. Madam, 'tis confess'd;
But what infer you from it?
190   *Lady.* This my lord;
That as all wrongs, though thrust into one scale
Slide of themselves off, when right fills the other,
And cannot bide the trial: so all wealth
(I mean if ill acquired), cemented to honour
195 By virtuous ways achiev'd, and bravely purchas'd,
Is but as rubbish pour'd into a river
(Howe'er intended to make good the bank)
Rend'ring the water that was pure before,
Polluted, and unwholesome. I allow
200 The heir of Sir Giles Overreach, Margaret,
A maid well qualifi'd, and the richest match
Our north part can make boast of, yet she cannot
With all that she brings with her fill their mouths,
That never will forget who was her father;
Or that my husband Alworth's lands, and
205   Welborne's
(How wrung from both needs now no repetition)
Were real motive, that more work'd your lordship
To join your families, than her form, and virtues;
You may conceive the rest.
    Lovell. I do sweet madam;
210 And long since have consider'd it. I know
The sum of all that makes a just man happy
Consists in the well choosing of his wife;
And there, well to discharge it, does require
Equality of years, of birth, of fortune;
215 For beauty being poor, and not cried up
By birth or wealth, can truly mix with neither.
And wealth, where there's such difference in years,
And fair descent, must make the yoke uneasy:
But I come nearer.
    Lady. Pray you do my lord.
    Lovell. Were Overreach' 'states thrice centupl'd;
220   his daughter

199 *allow* grant   203 *fill their mouths* silence them
209 *conceive the rest* supply the rest of my argument
215 *cried up* extolled, raised up
219 *come nearer* speak more particularly

Millions of degrees much fairer than she is,
(Howe'er I might urge precedents to excuse me)
I would not so adulterate my blood
By marrying Margaret, and so leave my issue
Made up of several pieces, one part scarlet   225
And the other London-blue. In my own tomb
I will inter my name first.
    Lady (aside). I am glad to hear this:
Why then my lord pretend you marriage to her?
Dissimulation but ties false knots
On that straight line, by which you hitherto   230
Have measur'd all your actions.
    Lovell. I make answer
And aptly, with a question. Wherefore have you,
That since your husband's death, have liv'd a strict,
And chaste nun's life, on the sudden giv'n yourself
To visits, and entertainments? Think you madam   235
'Tis not grown public conference? or the favours
Which you too prodigally have thrown on Welborne
Being too reserv'd before, incur not censure?
    Lady. I am innocent here, and on my life I swear
My ends are good.
    Lovell. On my soul so are mine   240
To Margaret: but leave both to the event.
And since this friendly privacy does serve
But as an offer'd means unto ourselves
To search each other farther; you having shown
Your care of me, I my respect to you;   245
Deny me not, but still in chaste words madam,
An afternoon's discourse.
    Lady. So I shall hear you.   *[Exeunt.]*

Act IV, Scene ii

Enter TAPWELL, FROTH

Tapwell. Undone, undone! this was your counsel,
    Froth.

222 *to excuse me* to justify my marrying beneath my rank
226 *London-blue* servants' livery
236 *public conference* common gossip
243 *offer'd means* welcome opportunity

Froth. Mine! I defy thee, did not Master Marrall
(He has marr'd all I am sure) strictly command us
(On pain of Sir Giles Overreach' displeasure)
To turn the gentleman out of doors?
5   *Tapwell.* 'Tis true;
But now he's his uncle's darling, and has got
Master Justice Greedy (since he fill'd his belly)
At his commandment, to do anything;
Woe, woe to us.
    Froth. He may prove merciful.
10   *Tapwell.* Troth, we do not deserve it at his hands:
Though he knew all the passages of our house;
As the receiving of stol'n goods, and bawdry,
When he was rogue Welborne, no man would believe
        him,
And then his information could not hurt us.
15   But now he is right worshipful again,
Who dares but doubt his testimony? me thinks
I see thee Froth already in a cart
For a close bawd, thine eyes ev'n pelted out
With dirt, and rotten eggs, and my hand hissing
20   (If I scape the halter) with the letter R,
Printed upon it.
    Froth. Would that were the worst:
That were but nine days' wonder; as for credit
We have none to lose; but we shall lose the money
He owes us and his custom, there's the hell on't.
    Tapwell. He has summon'd all his creditors by the
25   drum,
And they swarm about him like so many soldiers
On the pay day, and has found out such a new way
To pay his old debts, as 'tis very likely
He shall be chronicl'd for it.
    Froth. He deserves it
30   More than ten pageants. But are you sure his worship
Comes this way to my lady's?
        A cry within, 'Brave Master Welborne'.

---

11 *passages* goings-on   18 *close* secret
30 *pageants* triumphal processions (which the chronicles describe
    in detail)
31 *lady's* ed. (Q Ladies)

Tapwell. Yes I hear him.
Froth. Be ready with your petition and present it
To his good grace.

> *Enter* WELBORNE *in a rich habit,* GREEDY,
> [MARRALL], ORDER, FURNACE, *three* CREDITORS:
> TAPWELL *kneeling delivers his bill of debt.*

Welborne. How's this! petition'd too?
But note what miracles, the payment of
A little trash, and a rich suit of clothes   35
Can work upon these rascals. I shall be
I think Prince Welborne.
Marrall. When your worship's married
You may be, I know what I hope to see you.
Welborne. Then look thou for advancement.
Marrall. To be known
Your worship's bailiff is the mark I shoot at.   40
Welborne. And thou shalt hit it.
Marrall. Pray you sir dispatch
These needy followers, and for my admittance,
Provided you'll defend me from Sir Giles,
Whose service I am weary of, I'll say something
You shall give thanks for.
This interim, TAPWELL *and* FROTH *flattering and
bribing* JUSTICE GREEDY.
Welborne. Fear me not Sir Giles.   45
Greedy. Who? Tapwell? I remember thy wife
      brought me
Last New Year's tide, a couple of fat turkeys.
Tapwell. And shall do every Christmas, let your
      worship
But stand my friend now.
Greedy. How? With Master Welborne?
I can do any thing with him, on such terms;   50
See you this honest couple: they are good souls
As ever drew out fosset, have they not
A pair of honest faces?
Welborne. I o'erheard you,
And the bribe he promis'd, you are cozen'd in 'em,
For of all the scum that grew rich by my riots,   55

52 *drew out fosset* tapped a barrel

This for a most unthankful knave, and this
For a base bawd, and whore, have worst deserv'd me,
And therefore speak not for 'em, by your place
You are rather to do me justice; lend me your ear.
60   Forget his turkeys, and call in his licence,
And at the next fair, I'll give you a yoke of oxen
Worth all his poultry.
    Greedy. I am chang'd on the sudden
In my opinion! Come near; nearer rascal.
And now I view him better; did you e'er see
One look so like an arch-knave? his very
65   countenance,
Should an understanding judge but look on him,
Would hang him, though he were innocent.
    Tapwell, Froth. Worshipful sir.
    Greedy. No, though the great Turk came instead of
    turkeys,
To beg my favour, I am inexorable:
70   Thou hast an ill name: besides thy musty ale
That hath destroy'd many of the king's liege people,
Thou never hadst in thy house to stay men's stomachs
A piece of Suffolk cheese, or gammon of bacon,
Or any esculent, as the learned call it,
75   For their emolument, but sheer drink only.
For which gross fault, I here do damn thy licence,
Forbidding thee ever to tap, or draw.
For instantly, I will in mine own person
Command the constable to pull down thy sign;
And do it before I eat.
    Froth. No mercy?
80   *Greedy.* Vanish.
If I show any, may my promis'd oxen gore me.
    Tapwell. Unthankful knaves are ever so rewarded.
                  [*Exeunt* GREEDY, TAPWELL, FROTH.
    Welborne. Speak; what are you?
    1 Creditor. A decay'd vintner sir,
That might have thriv'd, but that your worship
       broke me

57 *deserv'd me* deserved at my hands
59 *ear* ed. (Q ear,)
74 *esculent* eatables   75 *emolument* benefit (fees)

With trusting you with muscadine and eggs,   85
And five-pound suppers, with your after drinkings,
When you lodg'd upon the Bankside.
 Welborne. I remember.
 1 Creditor. I have not been hasty, nor e'er laid to
  arrest you.
And therefore sir—
 Welborne. Thou art an honest fellow:
I'll set thee up again, see his bill paid.   90
What are you?
 2 Creditor. A tailor once, but now mere botcher.
I gave you credit for a suit of clothes,
Which was all my stock, but you failing in payment,
I was remov'd from the shop-board, and confin'd
Under a stall.
 Welborne. See him paid, and botch no more.   95
 2 Creditor. I ask no interest sir.
 Welborne. Such tailors need not,
If their bills are paid in one-and-twenty year
They are seldom losers. [*To* 3 CREDITOR.] O, I know
  thy face,
Thou wert my surgeon: you must tell no tales.
Those days are done. I will pay you in private.   100
 Order. A royal gentleman.
 Furnace. Royal as an emperor!
He'll prove a brave master, my good lady knew
To choose a man.
 Welborne. See all men else discharg'd.
And since old debts are clear'd by a new way,
A little bounty, will not misbecome me;   105
There's something honest cook for thy good
  breakfasts,
And this for your respect, take't, 'tis good gold
And I able to spare it.
 Order. You are too munificent.
 Furnace. He was ever so.
 Welborne. Pray you on before.

85 *muscadine* sweet wine
87 *Bankside* Southwark, the South bank of the Thames
87 *I remember* ed. (Q Remember)
88 *laid to arrest you* engaged serjeants to arrest you
91 *botcher* repairer, patcher

3 Creditor. Heaven bless you.
    Marrall. At four o'clock the rest know where to
110   meet me.
                        [*Exeunt* ORDER, FURNACE, CREDITORS.
    Welborne. Now Master Marrall, what's the weighty
        secret
You promis'd to impart?
    Marrall. Sir, time, nor place
Allow me to relate each circumstance;
This only in a word: I know Sir Giles
115 Will come upon you for security
For his thousand pounds, which you must not
        consent to.
As he grows in heat, as I am sure he will,
Be you but rough, and say he's in your debt
Ten times the sum, upon sale of your land;
120 I had a hand in't (I speak it to my shame)
When you were defeated of it.
    Welborne. That's forgiven.
    Marrall. I shall deserve't; then urge him to produce
The deed in which you pass'd it over to him,
Which I know he'll have about him to deliver
125 To the Lord Lovell, with many other writings,
And present moneys. I'll instruct you further,
As I wait on your worship, if I play not my prize
To your full content, and your uncle's much vexation,
Hang up Jack Marrall.
    Welborne. I rely upon thee.   [*Exeunt.*

Act IV, Scene iii

Enter ALWORTH, MARGARET.

    Alworth. Whether to yield the first praise to my
        lord's
Unequall'd temperance, or your constant sweetness,
That I yet live, my weak hands fasten'd on

121 *defeated* deprived
122 *deserve't; then* ed. (Q deserve't then;)
127 *play my prize* ed. (Q price) do my part, put up a good show
  1 *Whether* ed. (Q Whither)

Hope's anchor, spite of all storms of despair,
I yet rest doubtful.
  Margaret. Give it to Lord Lovell.   5
For what in him was bounty, in me's duty.
I make but payment of a debt, to which
My vows in that high office register'd
Are faithful witnesses.
  Alworth. 'Tis true my dearest,
Yet when when I call to mind how many fair ones   10
Make wilful shipwreck of their faiths, and oaths
To God and man, to fill the arms of greatness,
And you rise up no less than a glorious star
To the amazement of the world, that hold out
Against the stern authority of a father,   15
And spurn at honour when it comes to court you,
I am so tender of your good, that faintly
With your wrong I can wish myself that right
You yet are pleas'd to do me.
  Margaret. Yet, and ever.
To me what's title, when content is wanting?   20
Or wealth rak'd up together with much care,
And to be kept with more, when the heart pines,
In being dispossess'd of what it longs for,
Beyond the Indian mines; or the smooth brow
Of a pleas'd sire, that slaves me to his will?   25
And so his ravenous humour may be feasted
By my obedience, and he see me great,
Leaves to my soul nor faculties, nor power
To make her own election.
  Alworth. But the dangers
That follow the repulse—
  Margaret. To me they are nothing: 30
Let Alworth love, I cannot be unhappy.
Suppose the worst, that in his rage he kill me,
A tear, or two, by you dropp'd on my hearse
In sorrow for my fate, will call back life
So far, as but to say that I die yours,   35
I then shall rest in peace; or should he prove

8 *that high office* heaven
13 *rise up no less than* ed. (Q rise up less than)
30 *repulse*— ed. (Q repulse.)

So cruel, as one death would not suffice
His thirst of vengeance, but with ling'ring torments
In mind, and body, I must waste to air,
40   In poverty, join'd with banishment, so you share
In my afflictions (which I dare not wish you,
So high I prize you), I could undergo 'em
With such a patience as should look down
With scorn on his worst malice.
        Alworth. Heaven avert
45   Such trials of your true affection to me,
Nor will it unto you that are all mercy
Show so much rigour: but since we must run
Such desperate hazards, let us do our best
To steer between 'em.
        Margaret. Your lord's ours, and sure;
50   And though but a young actor second me
In doing to the life, what he has plotted,

        (*Enter* OVERREACH.)

The end may yet prove happy: now my Alworth.
        Alworth. To your letter, and put on a seeming
            anger.
        Margaret. I'll pay my lord all debts due to his title,
55   And when with terms, not taking from his honour,
He does solicit me, I shall gladly hear him.
But in this peremptory, nay commanding way,
T'appoint a meeting, and without my knowledge:
A priest to tie the knot, can ne'er be undone
60   Till death unloose it, is a confidence
In his lordship, will deceive him.
        Alworth. I hope better,
Good lady.
        Margaret. Hope sir what you please: for me
I must take a safe and secure course; I have
A father, and without his full consent,
65   Though all lords of the land kneel'd for my favour,
I can grant nothing.
        Overreach. I like this obedience,
But whatsoever my lord writes, must, and shall be

40 *so* provided that   46 *it* heaven
49 *ours* on our side

Accepted, and embrac'd. Sweet master Alworth,
You show yourself a true, and faithful servant
To your good lord, he has a jewel of you.   70
How? frowning Meg? are these looks to receive
A messenger from my lord? what's this? give me it.
   Margaret. A piece of arrogant paper like th'
      inscriptions.
              OVERREACH *read the letter.*
   Overreach. 'Fair Mistress from your servant learn,
      all joys
That we can hope for, if deferr'd, prove toys;   75
Therefore this instant, and in private meet
A husband, that will gladly at your feet
Lay down his honours, tend'ring them to you
With all content, the church being paid her due.'
Is this the arrogant piece of paper? Fool,   80
Will you still be one? in the name of madness, what
Could his good honour write more to content you?
Is there aught else to be wish'd after these two,
That are already offer'd? marriage first,
And lawful pleasure after: what would you more?   85
   Margaret. Why sir, I would be married like your
      daughter;
Not hurried away i'th'night I know not whither,
Without all ceremony: no friends invited
To honour the solemnity.
   Alworth. An't please your honour,
For so before tomorrow I must style you: 90
My lord desires this privacy in respect
His honourable kinsmen are far off,
And his desires to have it done brook not
So long delay as to expect their coming;
And yet he stands resolv'd, with all due pomp,   95
As running at the ring, plays, masques, and tilting,
To have his marriage at court celebrated
When he has brought your honour up to London.

70 *of you* in you
75 *toys* vanities   81 *still* always
91 *desires* ed. (Q desire); *in respect* because, seeing that
94 *expect* await
96 *running at the ring* thrusting a lance through a hanging ring
while riding at speed

  Overreach. He tells you true; 'tis the fashion on my
   knowledge.
100 Yet the good lord to please your peevishness
  Must put it off forsooth, and lose a night
  In which perhaps he might get two boys on thee.
  Tempt me no farther, if you do, this goad
  Shall prick you to him.
  Margaret. I could be contented,
105 Were you but by to do a father's part,
  And give me in the church.
  Overreach. So my lord have you
  What do I care who gives you? Since my lord
  Does purpose to be private, I'll not cross him.
  I know not Master Alworth how my lord
110 May be provided, and therefore there's a purse
  Of gold will serve this night's expense, tomorrow
  I'll furnish him with any sums: in the mean time
  Use my ring to my chaplain; he is benefic'd
  At my manor of Gotham, and call'd Parson Will-do.
115 'Tis no matter for a licence, I'll bear him out in't.
  Margaret. With your favour sir, what warrant is
   your ring?
  He may suppose I got that twenty ways
  Without your knowledge, and then to be refus'd,
  Were such a stain upon me, **if** you pleas'd sir
  Your presence would do better.
120 *Overreach.* Still perverse?
  I say again I will not cross my lord,
  Yet I'll prevent you too. Paper and ink there!
  Alworth. I can furnish you.
  Overreach. I thank you, I can write then.
          Writes on his book.
  Alworth. You may if you please, put out the name
   of my lord
125 In respect he comes disguis'd, and only write
  'Marry her to this gentleman'.

103 *goad* ed. (Q good) his sword
107 *gives you? Since* ed. (Q gives you, since)
119 *Were* ed. (Q We're)
122 *prevent you* anticipate your objections; *there!* ed. (Q there?)

Overreach. Well advis'd.

'Tis done, away, (MARGARET *kneels*.) my blessing girl?
    thou hast it.

Nay, no reply, begone, good Master Alworth,

This shall be the best night's work, you ever made.
    Alworth. I hope so sir.

                   [Exeunt ALWORTH *and* MARGARET.

    Overreach. Farewell, now all's cock-sure: 130

Methinks I hear already, knights, and ladies,

Say Sir Giles Overreach, how is it with

Your honourable daughter? has her honour

Slept well tonight? or will her honour please

To accept this monkey? dog? or paraquit?   135

(This is state in ladies) or my eldest son

To be her page, and wait upon her trencher?

My ends! my ends are compass'd! then for Welborne

And the lands; were he once married to the widow,

I have him here, I can scarce contain myself,   140

I am so full of joy; nay joy all over.

                [Exit. The end of the fourth act.

Act V, Scene i

Enter LOVELL, LADY, AMBLE. *[Exit* AMBLE.]

Lady. By this you know, how strong the motives
    were

That did, my lord, induce me to dispense

A little with my gravity, to advance

(In personating some few favours to him)

The plots, and projects of the down-trod Welborne.   5

Nor shall I e'er repent (although I suffer

In some few men's opinions for't) the action.

For he, that ventur'd all for my dear husband,

Might justly claim an obligation from me

To pay him such a courtesy: which had I   10

---

130 *cock-sure* secure, fixed, safe   135 *paraquit* parakeet
136 *state* a mark of dignity
s.d. *Exit. The end* ed. (Q Exit the end)
  4 *personating* feigning

Coyly, or over-curiously denied,
It might have argu'd me of little love
To the deceas'd.

    Lovell. What you intended madam
For the poor gentleman, hath found good success,
15 For as I understand his debts are paid,
And he once more furnish'd for fair employment.
But all the arts that I have us'd to raise
The fortunes of your joy, and mine, young Alworth,
Stand yet in supposition, though I hope well;
20 For the young lovers are in wit more pregnant
Than their years can promise; and for their desires,
On my knowledge they are equal.

    Lady. As my wishes
Are with yours my lord, yet give me leave to fear
The building though well grounded: to deceive
25 Sir Giles, that's both a lion, and a fox
In his proceedings, were a work beyond
The strongest undertakers, not the trial
Of two weak innocents.

    Lovell. Despair not madam:
Hard things are compass'd oft by easy means,
30 And judgement, being a gift deriv'd from heaven,
Though sometimes lodg'd i'th'hearts of worldly
       men
(That ne'er consider from whom they receive it)
Forsakes such as abuse the giver of it.
Which is the reason, that the politic,
35 And cunning statesman, that believes he fathoms
The counsels of all kingdoms on the earth,
Is by simplicity oft overreach'd.

    Lady. May he be so, yet in his name to express it
Is a good omen.

    Lovell. May it to myself
40 Prove so good lady in my suit to you:
What think you of the motion?

    Lady. Troth my lord
My own unworthiness may answer for me;
For had you, when that I was in my prime,

11 *over-curiously* too scrupulously
37 *overreach'd* ed. (Q overreach)   41 *motion* proposal

My virgin-flower uncropp'd, presented me
With this great favour, looking on my lowness   45
Not in a glass of self-love, but of truth,
I could not but have thought it as a blessing
Far, far beyond my merit.
   Lovell. You are too modest,
And undervalue that which is above
My title, or whatever I call mine.   50
I grant, were I a Spaniard, to marry
A widow might disparage me, but being
A true-born Englishman, I cannot find
How it can taint my honour; nay what's more,
That which you think a blemish is to me   55
The fairest lustre. You already madam
Have given sure proofs how dearly you can cherish
A husband that deserves you: which confirms me,
That if I am not wanting in my care
To do you service, you'll be still the same   60
That you were to your Alworth; in a word
Our years, our states, our births are not unequal,
You being descended nobly and alli'd so.
If then you may be won to make me happy,
But join your lips to mine, and that shall be   65
A solemn contract.
   Lady. I were blind to my own good
Should I refuse it, yet my lord receive me
As such a one, the study of whose whole life
Shall know no other object but to please you.
   Lovell. If I return not with all tenderness,   70
Equal respect to you, may I die wretched.
   Lady. There needs no protestation my lord
To her that cannot doubt—(*Enter* WELBORNE) You are
     welcome sir.
Now you look like yourself.
   Welborne. And will continue
Such in my free acknowledgement, that I am   75
Your creature madam, and will never hold
My life mine own, when you please to command it.
   Lovell. It is a thankfulness that well becomes you;
You could not make choice of a better shape,

63 *so.* ed. (Q so,)   73 *doubt*— ed. (Q doubt,)

To dress your mind in.
80   *Lady.* For me I am happy
That my endeavours prosper'd; saw you of late
Sir Giles, your uncle?
     Welborne. I heard of him, madam,
By his minister Marrall, he's grown into strange
     passions
About his daughter, this last night he look'd for
85 Your lordship at his house, but missing you,
And she not yet appearing, his wise head
Is much perplex'd, and troubl'd.
     Lovell. It may be
Sweetheart, my project took.
     Lady. I strongly hope.

> *Enter* OVERREACH, *with distracted looks, driving
> in* MARRALL *before him.*

Overreach. Ha! find her booby thou huge lump of
     nothing;
I'll bore thine eyes out else.
90   *Welborne.* May it please your lordship
For some ends of mine own but to withdraw
A little out of sight, though not of hearing,
You may perhaps have sport.
     Lovell. You shall direct me.   *Steps aside.*
     Overreach. I shall sol fa you rogue.
     Marrall. Sir, for what cause
Do you use me thus?
95   *Overreach.* Cause, slave? why I am angry,
And thou a subject only fit for beating,
And so to cool my choler, look to the writing;
Let but the seal be broke upon the box
That has slept in my cabinet these three years,
I'll rack thy soul for't.
100 *Marrall* (*aside*). I may yet cry quittance,
Though now I suffer, and dare not resist.
     Overreach. Lady, by your leave, did you see my
          daughter lady?
And the lord her husband? Are they in your house?
If they are, discover, that I may bid 'em joy;

83 *minister* agent.   94 *sol fa* make you 'sing' (with pain).

And as an entrance to her place of honour,   105
Set your ladyship on her left hand, and make
    curtseys
When she nods on you; which you must receive
As a special favour.
    Lady. When I know, Sir Giles,
Her state requires such ceremony, I shall pay it;
But in the mean time, as I am myself,   110
I give you to understand, I neither know,
Nor care where her honour is.
    Overreach. When you once see her
Supported, and led by the lord her husband
You'll be taught better. Nephew.
    Welborne. Sir.
    Overreach. No more?
    Welborne. 'Tis all I owe you.
    Overreach. Have your redeem'd rags   115
Made you thus insolent?
    Welborne (in scorn). Insolent to you?
Why what are you sir, unless in your years,
At the best more than myself?
    Overreach. His fortune swells him;
'Tis rank he's married.
    Lady. This is excellent!
    Overreach. Sir, in calm language (though I seldom
    use it),   120
I am familiar with the cause, that makes you
Bear up thus bravely, there's a certain buzz
Of a stol'n marriage, do you hear? of a stol'n marriage,
In which 'tis said there's somebody hath been cozen'd.
I name no parties.
    Welborne. Well sir, and what follows?   125
    Overreach. Marry this; since you are peremptory:
    remember
Upon mere hope of your great match, I lent you
A thousand pounds: put me in good security,
And suddenly, by mortgage, or by statute,

106 *Set* ed. (Q See); *curtseys* ed. (Q courseis)
109 *state* station   115 *Overreach.* ed. (Q *Welb.*)
119 *rank* obvious   122 *buzz* rumour
123 *hear? of a stol'n marriage,* ed. (Q heare of a stolne marriage?)
129 *by mortgage* ed. (Q my Mortgage)

130 Of some of your new possessions, or I'll have you
Dragg'd in your lavender robes to the gaol, you
     know me,
And therefore do not trifle.
    Welborne. Can you be
So cruel to your nephew? now he's in
The way to rise: was this the courtesy
135 You did me in pure love, and no ends else?
    Overreach. End me no ends: engage the whole estate,
And force your spouse to sign it, you shall have
Three or four thousand more to roar, and swagger,
And revel in bawdy taverns.
    Welborne. And beg after:
Mean you not so?
140   *Overreach.* My thoughts are mine, and free.
Shall I have security?
    Welborne. No: indeed you shall not:
Nor bond, nor bill, nor bare acknowledgement,
Your great looks fright not me.
    Overreach. But my deeds shall:
Outbrav'd?   *They both draw, the* SERVANTS *enter.*
    Lady. Help murder, murder.
    Welborne. Let him come on,
145 With all his wrongs, and injuries about him,
Arm'd with his cut-throat practices to guard him;
The right that I bring with me, will defend me,
And punish his extortion.
    Overreach. That I had thee
But single in the field.
    Lady. You may, but make not
My house your quarrelling scene.
150   *Overreach.* Were't in a church
By heaven, and hell, I'll do't.
    Marrall. Now put him to
The showing of the deed.
    Welborne. This rage is vain sir;
For fighting fear not you shall have your hands full,
Upon the least incitement; and whereas
155 You charge me with a debt of a thousand pounds,
If there be law, (howe'er you have no conscience)

131 *lavender robes* robes recently 'laid in lavender', *i.e.* pawned

Either restore my land, or I'll recover
A debt, that's truly due to me, from you
In value ten times more than what you challenge.
    Overreach. I in thy debt! O impudence! did I not
        purchase   160
The land left by thy father? that rich land,
That had continued in Welborne's name
Twenty descents; which like a riotous fool
Thou didst make sale of? Is not here enclos'd
The deed that does confirm it mine?
    Marrall. Now, now.   165
    Welborne. I do acknowledge none, I ne'er pass'd
        o'er
Any such land. I grant for a year, or two,
You had it in trust, which if you do discharge,
Surrend'ring the possession, you shall ease
Yourself, and me, of chargeable suits in law,   170
Which if you prove not honest, (as I doubt it)
Must of necessity follow.
    Lady. In my judgement
He does advise you well.
    Overreach. Good! good! conspire
With your new husband lady; second him
In his dishonest practices; but when   175
This manor is extended to my use,
You'll speak in an humbler key, and sue for favour.
    Lady. Never: do not hope it.
    Welborne. Let despair first seize me.
    Overreach. Yet to shut up thy mouth, and make thee
        give
Thyself the lie, the loud lie: I draw out   180
The precious evidence; if thou canst forswear
Thy hand, and seal, and make a forfeit of
                          (*Opens the box.*)
Thy ears to the pillory: see here's that will make
My interest clear. Ha!
    Lady. A fair skin of parchment.
    Welborne. Indented I confess, and labels too,   185
But neither wax, nor words. How! thunder-struck?
Not a syllable to insult with? my wise uncle,

177 *extended* legally seized

Is this your precious evidence? is this that makes
Your interest clear?

Overreach. I am o'erwhelm'd with wonder!
190 What prodigy is this, what subtle devil
Hath raz'd out the inscription, the wax
Turn'd into dust! the rest of my deeds whole,
As when they were deliver'd! and this only
Made nothing! do you deal with witches rascal?
195 There is a statute for you, which will bring
Your neck in a hempen circle, yes, there is;
And now 'tis better thought for, cheater know
This juggling shall not save you.

Welborne. To save thee
Would beggar the stock of mercy.

Overreach. Marrall.

Marrall. Sir.

Overreach (*flattering him*). Though the witnesses are
200   dead, your testimony
Help with an oath or two, and for thy master,
Thy liberal master, my good honest servant,
I know, you will swear anything to dash
This cunning sleight: besides, I know thou art
205 A public notary, and such stand in law
For a dozen witnesses; the deed being drawn too
By thee, my careful Marrall, and deliver'd
When thou wert present will make good my title.
Wilt thou not swear this?

Marrall. I? No I assure you.
210 I have a conscience, not sear'd up like yours.
I know no deeds.

Overreach. Wilt thou betray me?

Marrall. Keep him
From using of his hands, I'll use my tongue
To his no little torment.

Overreach. Mine own varlet
Rebel against me?

Marrall. Yes, and uncase you too.
215 The idiot; the patch; the slave; the booby;

189 *interest* title, legal right
197 *thought for, cheater* ed. (Q thought, for Cheater)
202 *servant,* ed. (Q servant.)   214 *uncase* strip, expose

The property fit only to be beaten
For your morning exercise; your football, or
Th'unprofitable lump of flesh; your drudge
Can now anatomize you, and lay open
All your black plots; and level with the earth   220
Your hill of pride; and with these gabions guarded,
Unload my great artillery, and shake,
Nay pulverize the walls you think defend you.
    Lady. How he foams at the mouth with rage.
    Welborne. To him again.
    Overreach. O that I had thee in my gripe, I would
            tear thee   225
Joint after joint.
    Marrall. I know you are a tearer,
But I'll have first your fangs par'd off, and then
Come nearer to you, when I have discover'd,
And made it good before the judge, what ways
And devilish practices you us'd to cozen   230
An army of whole families, who yet live,
And but enroll'd for soldiers were able
To take in Dunkirk.
    Welborne. All will come out.
    Lady. The better.
    Overreach. But that I will live, rogue, to torture
            thee,
And make thee wish, and kneel in vain to die,   235
These swords that keep thee from me, should fix here,
Although they made my body but one wound,
But I would reach thee.
    Lovell (aside). Heav'n's hand is in this,
One bandog worry the other.
    Overreach. I play the fool,
And make my anger but ridiculous.   240
There will be a time, and place, there will be cowards,
When you shall feel what I dare do.
    Welborne. I think so:

216 *property* handy object   219 *anatomize* dissect
222 *gabions* baskets filled with earth for fortifications; here meta-
phorically for Welborne and the servants
231 *An* ed. (Q With an)
233 *take in* capture
236 *here* in my breast
239 *bandog* fierce dog kept tied

You dare do any ill, yet want true valour
To be honest, and repent.
   Overreach. They are words I know not,
245 Nor e'er will learn. Patience, the beggar's virtue,
                    (*Enter* GREEDY *and* PARSON WILL-DO.)
Shall find no harbour here; after these storms
At length a calm appears. Welcome, most welcome:
There's comfort in thy looks, is the deed done?
Is my daughter married? say but so my chaplain
And I am tame.
250   *Will-do.* Married? Yes I assure you.
   Overreach. Then vanish all sad thoughts; there's
       more gold for thee.
My doubts, and fears are in the titles drown'd
Of my honourable, my right honourable daughter.
   Greedy. Here will be feasting; at least for a month
255 I am provided: empty guts croak no more,
You shall be stuff'd like bagpipes, not with wind
But bearing dishes.
   Overreach (*whispering to* WILL-DO). Instantly be
      here?
To my wish, to my wish, now you that plot against me,
And hop'd to trip my heels up; that contemn'd me;
                         (*Loud Music*).
260 Think on't and tremble, they come I hear the music.
A lane there for my lord.
   Welborne. This sudden heat
May yet be cool'd sir.
   Overreach. Make way there for my lord.

          Enter ALWORTH *and* MARGARET.

   Margaret (*kneeling*). Sir, first your pardon, then your
      blessing, with
Your full allowance of the choice I have made.
265 As ever you could make use of your reason,
Grow not in passion: since you may as well
Call back the day that's past, as untie the knot
Which is too strongly fasten'd, not to dwell

253 *Of my honourable* ed. (Q Of my right honorable)
254 *Here will be* ed. (Q Here will I be)
257 *bearing dishes* substantial, well-weighted dishes

Too long on words, this is my husband.

   Overreach. How!

   Alworth. So I assure you: all the rites of marriage   270
With every circumstance are past, alas sir,
Although I am no lord, but a lord's page,
Your daughter, and my lov'd wife mourns not for it.
And for right honourable son-in-law, you may say
Your dutiful daughter.

   Overreach. Devil: are they married?   275

   Will-do. Do a father's part, and say heav'n give 'em
    joy.

   Overreach. Confusion, and ruin, speak and speak
    quickly,
Or thou art dead.

   Will-do. They are married.

   Overreach. Thou hadst better
Have made a contract with the king of fiends
Than these, my brain turns!

   Will-do. Why this rage to me?   280
Is not this your letter sir? and these the words?
Marry her to this gentleman.

   Overreach. It cannot:
Nor will I e'er believe it, 'sdeath I will not,
That I, that in all passages I touch'd
At worldly profit, have not left a print   285
Where I have trod for the most curious search
To trace my footsteps, should be gull'd by children,
Baffl'd, and fool'd, and all my hopes, and labours,
Defeated, and made void.

   Welborne. As it appears
You are so my grave uncle.

   Overreach. Village nurses   290
Revenge their wrongs with curses, I'll not waste
A syllable, but thus I take the life
Which wretched I gave to thee.

                Offers to kill MARGARET.

   Lovell. Hold for your own sake!
Though charity to your daughter hath quite left you,
Will you do an act, though in your hopes lost here,   295

283 *it, 'sdeath* ed. (Q it's death)   293 *wretched I* my wretched self
293 *sake!* ed. (Q sake)   295 *here* on earth

Can leave no hope for peace, or rest hereafter?
Consider; at the best you are but a man,
And cannot so create your aims, but that
They may be cross'd.
    Overreach. Lord, thus I spit at thee,
300 And at thy counsel; and again desire thee
And as thou art a soldier, if thy valour
Dares show itself where multitude, and example
Lead not the way, let's quit the house, and change
Six words in private.
    Lovell. I am ready.
    Lady. Stay sir.
Contest with one distracted?
305   *Welborne.* You'll grow like him
Should you answer his vain challenge.
    Overreach. Are you pale?
Borrow his help, though Hercules call it odds
I'll stand against both, as I am hemm'd in thus.
Since like a Lybian lion in the toil,
310 My fury cannot reach the coward hunters
And only spends itself, I'll quit the place.
Alone I can do nothing: but I have servants
And friends to second me, and if I make not
This house a heap of ashes (by my wrongs,
315 What I have spoke I will make good), or leave
One throat uncut, if it be possible
Hell add to my afflictions.   [*Exit* OVERREACH.
    Marrall. Is't not brave sport?
    Greedy. Brave sport? I am sure it has ta'en away
      my stomach;
I do not like the sauce.
    Alworth. Nay, weep not dearest:
320 Though it express your pity, what's decreed
Above, we cannot alter.
    Lady. His threats move me
No scruple, madam.
    Marrall. Was it not a rare trick
(And it please your worship) to make the deed nothing?
I can do twenty neater, if you please

296 *hereafter* after death   300 *again* in return
309 *like a* ed. (Q like)   315 *leave* ed. (Q leau'd)

To purchase, and grow rich, for I will be   325
Such a solicitor, and steward for you,
As never worshipful had.
    Welborne. I do believe thee.
But first discover the quaint means you us'd
To raze out the conveyance?
    Marrall. They are mysteries
Not to be spoke in public: certain minerals   330
Incorporated in the ink, and wax.
Besides he gave me nothing, but still fed me
With hopes, and blows; and that was the inducement
To this conundrum. If it please your worship
To call to memory, this mad beast once caus'd me   335
To urge you, or to drown, or hang yourself;
I'll do the like to him if you command me.
    Welborne. You are a rascal, he that dares be false
To a master, though unjust, will ne'er be true
To any other: look not for reward,   340
Or favour from me, I will shun thy sight
As I would do a basilisk's. Thank my pity
If thou keep thy ears, howe'er I will take order
Your practice shall be silenc'd.
    Greedy. I'll commit him,
If you'll have me sir?
    Welborne. That were to little purpose;   345
His conscience be his prison, not a word
But instantly begone.
    Order. Take this kick with you.
    Amble. And this.
    Furnace. If that I had my cleaver here
I would divide your knave's head.
    Marrall. This is the haven
False servants still arrive at.   [*Exit* MARRALL.

Enter OVERREACH.

    Lady. Come again.   350
    Lovell. Fear not I am your guard.
    Welborne. His looks are ghastly.

329 *conveyance* title-deed   331 *wax.* ed. (Q wax?)
342 *basilisk* legendary reptile which destroyed by a look

Will-do. Some little time I have spent (under your
    favours)
In physical studies, and if my judgement err not
He's mad beyond recovery: but observe him,
And look to yourselves.
355   *Overreach.* Why, is not the whole world
Included in my self? to what use then
Are friends, and servants? say there were a squadron
Of pikes, lin'd through with shot, when I am mounted,
Upon my injuries, shall I fear to charge 'em?
360 No: I'll through the battalia, and that routed,
I'll fall to execution.
        (Flourishing his sword unsheathed.)
        Ha! I am feeble:
Some undone widow sits upon mine arm,
And takes away the use of't; and my sword
Glu'd to my scabbard, with wrong'd orphans' tears,
365 Will not be drawn. Ha! what are these? sure hangmen,
That come to bind my hands, and then to drag me
Before the judgement seat; now they are new shapes
And do appear like furies, with steel whips
To scourge my ulcerous soul; shall I then fall.
370 Ingloriously, and yield? no, spite of fate,
I will be forc'd to hell like to myself,
Though you were legions of accursed spirits,
Thus would I fly among you.
    Welborne. There's no help;
Disarm him first, then bind him.
    Greedy. Take a mittimus
And carry him to Bedlam.
375   *Lovell.* How he foams!
    Welborne. And bites the earth.
    Will-do. Carry him to some dark room,
There try what art can do for his recovery.
    Margaret. O my dear father!
                [*They force* OVERREACH *off.*

353 *physical studies* medical studies
358 *lin'd through with shot* reinforced with musketeers
373 *Thus* ed. (Q *Welb.* Thus); Welborne. *There's* ed. (Q There's)
374 *mittimus* justice's warrant for confinement
375 *Bedlam* a hospital for lunatics

Alworth. You must be patient mistress.

Lovell. Here is a precedent to teach wicked men
That when they leave religion, and turn atheists   380
Their own abilities leave 'em; pray you take comfort;
I will endeavour you shall be his guardians
In his distractions: and for your land Master Welborne,
Be it good, or ill in law, I'll be an umpire,
Between you, and this, th'undoubted heir   385
Of Sir Giles Overreach; for me, here's the anchor
That I must fix on.

Alworth. What you shall determine,
My lord, I will allow of.

Welborne. 'Tis the language
That I speak too; but there is something else
Beside the repossession of my land,   390
And payment of my debts, that I must practise.
I had a reputation, but 'twas lost
In my loose courses; and till I redeem it
Some noble way, I am but half made up.
It is a time of action; if your lordship   395
Will please to confer a company upon me
In your command, I doubt not in my service
To my king, and country, but I shall do something
That may make me right again.

Lovell. Your suit is granted,
And you lov'd for the motion.

Welborne. Nothing wants then   400
But your allowance.

382 *you* Margaret and Alworth
386 *the anchor* Lady Alworth
393 *courses* ed. (Q course)
401 *your allowance* the spectators' approval

THE EPILOGUE

But your allowance, and in that, our all
Is comprehended; it being known, nor we
Nor he that wrote the comedy can be free
Without your manumission, which if you
405   Grant willingly, as a fair favour due
To the poet's and our labours (as you may,
For we despair not gentlemen of the play),
We jointly shall profess your grace hath might
To teach us action, and him how to write.

FINIS

404 *manumission* setting at liberty (here, by applause)
408 *grace* graciousness, kindness
409 *action* acting

NOTES

SIR HENRY MOODY'S VERSES
3-7. 'You have placed in your debt the present age, posterity, the theatre, and the original audience.'
11-14. 'Only those too stupid to understand the play have escaped becoming your debtors.'

DRAMATIS PERSONAE

The spelling of the names follows Q. To print 'Wellborn' and 'Allworth' would perhaps encourage an unnaturally precise pronunciation of the names in order to bring out their meaning. They become accepted as ordinary surnames as the play proceeds. Only the 'Will-doe' of Q has been modernized, to prevent mispronunciation: Will-do's name, like that of Parson Supple in *Tom Jones*, implies pliability: *cf*. IV.iii, 114.

Welborne's Christian name is Francis or Frank (I.i, 39); Alworth's Tom (I.iii, 50); Marrall's Jack (II.iii, 9); and Tapwell's Timothy (I.i, 25). Greedy's name is treated throughout as his surname except at III.ii, 92, where, for the nonce, he says his name is Greedy Woodcock (see note).

6. *Term-driver*. The exact meaning of the word is not known. The Oxford English Dictionary conjectures that it is the same as term-trotter, 'one who comes up to the law courts for the term'. Wheeler conjectures 'one who insists on hard terms in a lease or other contract'. From the use of the word at II.ii, 121, I should guess it to be simply a derogatory synonym for 'Lawyer'.

I.i, s.d. Welborne is in ragged clothes, *cf*. lines 8, 17.
I.i, 1. The whole of this opening dialogue is in Jonson's manner: *cf. The Alchemist*, I.i.
I.i, 13. *A potent monarch, call'd the constable*. The mock-heroic strain here (*cf*. 'this sceptre', line 92)

recalls Beaumont and Fletcher's *The Knight of the Burning Pestle.*

I.i, 34, 35. A member of the *quorum* was one of the chief Justices of the Peace, whose presence was necessary to constitute a bench; the *custos rotulorum* or keeper of the rolls was the principal Justice.

I.i, 103-7. *'Tis a noble widow . . . envy, or detraction.* This is introduced so that we do not misinterpret her later behaviour to Welborne as Sir Giles does in III.iii.

I.i, 113-4. *I dare undertake . . . entertainment.* Alworth means simply that his mother will entertain Welborne in spite of his poverty; but the context perhaps suggests to Welborne the stratagem which he will later practise.

I.i, 131. *Does it blush?* Thus Q. 'It' as a personal pronoun was used familiarly, or (as here) mock-contemptuously. Some editors read 'Dost blush?', which is possibly right: for the compositor sometimes expands supposed contractions, and prints, *e.g.*, 'scall'd' for 'scald' (III.ii, 72) and 'slepp'd' for 'slept' (V.i, 90); he even prints 'fien'd' for 'fiend' (II.i, 121) and 'horri'd' for 'horrid' (III.i, 6). The forms 'you' and 'thou' are used indiscriminately in the scene and do not therefore help to establish the right reading.

I.i, 136-7. Alworth is just too old to be beaten for misbehaviour by the porter, but is still a page. Pages were ceremonially 'sworn in' on a slipper by other pages (see the 'induction' to Nashe's *Unfortunate Traveller*).

I.i, 155. *Tom, I must tell you.* 'True' is awkwardly placed in the line and adds little or nothing to the sense. Alworth uses Welborne's Christian name three times in this dialogue; one would expect Welborne to return the familiarity, as the older man. A compositor might mistake 'Tom' in MS for 'True'.

I.ii, 8-10. Anger was traditionally an occupational disease with cooks. Jonson, *The Alchemist* III.i, connects it, as Massinger does here, with the heat of the kitchen.

I.ii, 27. *Breda*. Besieged for ten months, 1624–1625, by Spanish forces under the Marquis of Spinola. Amble alludes in the next speech to the defenders' shortage of food.

I.ii, 48. *Our late young master*. Alworth was their 'young' master when his father lived.

I.ii, 53. *Her presence answer for us*. 'Let her presence answer for us.'

I.ii, 58. *A summer suit*. A witty antidote to Furnace's choler; *cf.* his reply 'Furnace now grows cool' (for the style of which *cf.* 'Pistol's cock is up', *Henry V*, II.i).

I.ii, 74–5. *His purpose / For the Low Countries*. Introduces the theme of military service abroad, leading ultimately to Welborne's recovery of his reputation.

I.ii, 86–8. *That . . . / Who . . .* Emendation is unnecessary: the irregular grammar would pass on the stage; *cf.* I.iii, 5, 'Which we that are her servants ought to serve it.'

I.ii, 100–14. A moral and rhetorical set-piece, characteristic of Massinger but not in his best style.

I.ii, 119. *I warn you*. The emendation is necessary. Lady Alworth has not previously forbidden Alworth to consort with Welborne. This explains his behaviour at I.iii, 50–1.

I.ii, 127. Q's 'You follow' was perhaps due to printing a word cancelled in manuscript.

I.iii, 30. *Henrici decimo quarto*. 'In the Statutes for the fourteenth year of Henry [VIII].' Pure pedantic fantasy.

I.iii, 44. *Pie-Corner*. A London street famous for its cooks' shops. The Nottinghamshire justice's play on words is wholly for the benefit of the London audience.

I.iii, 66. *My lady*. Order announces his lady's entry. Not a reply to Welborne's rhetorical question.

I.iii, 74. *These—*. Welborne presumably would have added 'injuries', if Lady Alworth had not interrupted him. The metre precludes a heavy stress on 'these', which it would need if 'these' meant 'these people' and ended the sentence, as it does in *The City-Madam*

(V.iii, 145), 'Those horrid ends to which thou didst design these.'

I.iii, 128-9. *Now what . . . in supposition.* Aside.

II.i. Editors localize this scene in 'A Room in Over-reach's House', but Welborne would not be admitted without Sir Giles's knowledge or permission (line 89, 'See, who's here, sir'). It takes place outdoors, when Overreach and Marrall are returning from the commission, and Welborne from Lady Alworth's house (which is 'not far off', line 140).

II.i, 2. *Your worship have the way on't.* 'You know the trick': a tribute to Sir Giles personally. Emendation to 'your worships' is wrong. Marrall's lines do not mean that Sir Giles sat on the commission (*cf.* lines 10–13 below; but *cf.* also I.iii, where he does seem to mean it, and perhaps we should emend to 'your worship' accordingly, to limit it to Greedy); they mean that he caused it to be held, as is explained in what follows.

II.i, 51. *This varlet Marrall lives too long.* 'Marrall' is vocative, and must not be changed to 'Welborne'.

II.i, 54-5. Massinger is master of the details of his plot: *cf.* IV.ii, 2-5.

II.i, 75-6. *And write honourable / Right honourable.* The words were not pronounced alike in Massinger's time; the phrase is awkward for the modern actor. For the expression, *cf.* 'Many for their wealth (I grant) / Have written ladies of honour' (*The City-Madam*, V.i, 94–5).

II.i, 81. *Come from the city.* Belong to the merchant class, not the aristocracy. He has his lands, and very likely his title, by purchase; not by descent. 89. *True gentry.* Massinger, not Overreach, is speaking here.

II.i, 120-2. 'Despair' was earlier used by Overreach (line 66) in the modern sense, of that which drives a man to desperate (rash and criminal) actions. Here Welborne's reference to the fiend suggests the theological sense of 'despair', that is, culpable hopelessness leading to suicide and the death of the soul.

In Elizabethan literature the ruined prodigal was a natural prey of despair, and is in some early plays tempted to suicide by a character called Despair.

II.i, 132. 'Not merely at her house but in her company.'

II.i, 142. Marrall expects Welborne to be literally tossed in a blanket by Lady Alworth's servants (a character is so treated in Massinger's *The Parliament of Love*, IV.v), or to be driven from the door with dog-whips.

II.ii, 15. *You hear my lady's charge.* The Q reading 'You are' is unsatisfactory; it probably occurred through a compositor's reading of 'You heare' as 'You he are', with consequent mistaken alteration.

II.ii, 17–26. 'Many of the ingredients of Furnace's cordial—a drink which stimulates the circulation—were also used for aphrodisiacs. The *double entendre* of Furnace's last three lines would not be lost on a contemporary audience, after the details of the elixir's ingredients.' (Byrne.)

II.ii, 34. Watchall here opens the door to admit Welborne and Marrall. The stage door is used, and there is no need for him to leave the stage and return. Alworth remains on stage, while the other servants 'go off several ways'.

II.ii, 60. *On Sundays.* For his Sunday dinner, his best meal of the week.

II.ii, 90. *Will you still be babbling?* A nice touch, showing Furnace's free-spoken manner once more, and throwing into relief Marrall's awkward respectfulness towards the lady.

II.ii, 108. *Bought of the hangman.* A hanged man's clothes were the hangman's perquisite.

II.ii, 123. *Ram-Alley.* A London street with cooks' shops. The allusion (*cf.* I.iii, 44, Pie-Corner) suits the audience rather than the characters and setting of the play.

II.ii, 133–7. Aside to Amble. Welborne and Marrall are standing at a distance. She returns to them at line 137, and by line 139 is in conversation with Welborne alone.

II.ii, 144. *Your worship.* Marrall's first use to Welborne

of a phrase which in the next scene will become his constant refrain, with a very comic effect in his following conversation with Sir Giles, II.iii, 78, 104.

II.iii. This scene, beginning with Marrall and Welborne, and ending with Marrall and Overreach, is the counterpart of II.i.

II.iii, 37. *Knave's-Acre*. An apt tenancy for Marrall. The phrase was traditional.

II.iii, 59, s.d. *Walk by musing*. Stage directions in the imperative usually, though not invariably, indicate the prompter's hand. There are other examples at III.ii, 218 and IV.iii, 73. Contrast also III.ii, 170, s.d., '*Exeunt omnes praeter* Overreach' with, a dozen lines later, line 182, s.d., '*The rest off*'.

II.iii, 60. *Sirrah, take my horse*. Addressed to a servant off stage.

II.iii, 82–4. The text still seems corrupt here, even after emendation.

II.iii, 90. *Though I came—a suitor*. A new piece of information. Massinger does well in revealing it casually now instead of systematically collecting it with the rest of the exposition.

II.iii, 94. *A dog that cannot blush*. Proverbial: usually a black dog.

II.iii, 96. *Buttermilk cheeks*. Marrall is beginning to show fear of Sir Giles's obvious anger.

II.iii, 109. *He's gone*. Should we add 'sir', to complete the metre, and express Marrall's servility?

II.iii, 109–11. A good change of subject from an 'imaginary feast, and lady' to a feast of real importance and a distinguished visitor.

III.i, s.d. The servants merely appear at the door after Lord Lovell and Alworth, and receive their instructions.

III.i, 17. *Guard*. 'Adorn' (Cruickshank, citing *King John* IV.iii, 10); but perhaps to be taken without metaphor, as meaning 'put on a modest blush in defence against a compliment'.

III.i, 21–8. Contrast Lord Lovell's behaviour with Sir

Giles's, both in what we have just seen of his relations with Marrall and in his arrogance in making decayed gentlewomen his daughter's servants. It is a pity that Lord Lovell must say this of himself, however.

III.i, 68–70. (*Such as if Ulysses . . . resist*). The syntax is confused but the meaning clear. The usual emendation ('such as Ulysses, if he . . .') repairs the grammar at the expense of the verse, which should stress 'Ulysses'.

III.i, 79. *Hippolytus*. Son of Theseus, tragically loved by his stepmother Phaedra. The type of masculine chastity.

III.i, 80–1. *Love hath made you / Poetical, Alworth.* We can afford a smile here, since we are sure enough that Alworth will marry Margaret at last. This is Massinger's way of keeping the rich sentiment of the scene from cloying. The touch of humour also gives Lord Lovell a maturity which contrasts well with Alworth's youthful romanticism; and it helps to make Alworth himself more credible.

III.i, 90–1. *Must, trust*. 'The rhyme is unintentional: Massinger hardly ever has rhyme, except at the end of a scene.' (Cruickshank). He uses it at IV.iii, 74, for Lord Lovell's letter, to mark it off from the surrounding dialogue.

III.ii, 15. *Almost as much as to give thanks for 'em.* Meaning that what he likes best is to have just eaten them; *cf.* lines 23–4. His role as kitchen overseer may derive from the *Captivi* of Plautus, where the parasite Ergasilus similarly officiates.

III.ii, 39. *Downefalne*. Downfallen. Two syllables.

III.ii, 74. *I'll give thanks for*. Thus Q, possibly as a relative clause with 'dumpling': most editors read 'for't', perhaps rightly.

III.ii, 91. Cruickshank cites references to the reputation of tailors as good eaters.

III.ii, 92. *And my name, though a justice, Greedy Woodcock.* A 'woodcock' is slang for a fool; a justice is proverbially wise. Greedy's name is treated as his surname throughout the rest of the play. He is here given the extra name of 'Woodcock' so that he can make the joke in the next line, a joke that had been made by Cob (on cob herrings) in Jonson's *Every Man In His Humour*, I.iii and II.ii.

III.ii, 108. *See you.* Look you; pay attention to this. Some editors delete the Q's comma and read 'see you do not coy it', but this detracts from the emphasis.

III.ii, 116–7. *Though he came / Like Jupiter to Semele.* That is, however hot and devouring his passion might be. Semele was destroyed by the sight of her lover in his full glory.

III.ii, 137. The Q reading can be defended grammatically but is neither good logic nor good metre. Editors usually emend to 'Whene'er tempted'. The present reading is closer to the Q. Perhaps the compositor misread 'his' as 'h'is'.

III.ii, 179, s.d. *They salute.* Lord Lovell kisses Margaret after she is presented to him in the following line.

III.ii, 180. *A black-brow'd girl.* Spoken apologetically, fair hair being more esteemed than dark. Overreach himself ('the Richard III of middling life', as Scott well described him) would be dark and sinister. Alworth is, one feels sure, blond.

III.ii, 186. *Remember—.* The double aspect of Overreach in this scene, his show of geniality and his underlying ruthlessness, offers a good opportunity to the actor.

III.ii, 199. *And tissues . . . suit but ill.* Tissue is silk interwoven with gold or silver; scarlet a fine worsted material (not always red). The point here is that the two fabrics are incompatible, rather than that each of them stands for a particular social class.

III.ii, 203, s.d. *Enter Greedy.* The comic effect of this is intensified, not weakened, by his earlier interruptions of Overreach's dialogue with Margaret. If Overreach was angry then, what must be his feelings now?

III.ii, 209. *Barathrum of the shambles.* From Horace, *Epistles*, I.xv, 31, 'barathrum macelli' (devouring gulf of the meat-market):

'the very bane
And ruin of the shambles; what he got

He swallow'd; all went down his greedy throat.'
(Creech's translation)

III.ii, 218, s.d. *Thrust Greedy off*. And, in view of the next direction at line 228, exit with him. This enables the rest of Lord Lovell's dialogue with Margaret to be spoken aloud without theatrical awkwardness.

III.ii, 242. *O my guts!* Spencer regards this as 'an actor's gag, the line being completed by the present line 243'. Half-lines, as Cruickshank notes here, are rare in Massinger. But Lady Alworth's half-line indicates a continuing conversation with Welborne. They cannot enter immediately after their coach is heard, and Greedy's completion of line 242 (and the actors' business which no doubt accompanies it) fills the gap. There is another extra-metrical speech at IV.i, 11, for Overreach off stage.

III.ii, 247. *And thus attended!* Welborne is still shabbily dressed, *cf.* line 269, so this entry would be striking, especially as Lady Alworth has come out of mourning (*cf.* III.iii, 3; she would be dressed in black earlier). This explains line 260, 'I borrow'd so much from my long restraint', as 'I ended my mourning a little before its due time'.

III.ii, 267. *If meat can do it*. A witty touch; *cf.* her offer of a summer suit to Furnace, and her ironical use of 'her honour' at V.i, 112.

III.ii, 288. *Pray you lead, we follow*. Spoken to Overreach, who thereupon offers his arm to Lady Alworth, thus producing her next line, in which 'you' and 'my' are to be stressed. She goes out with Welborne, while Greedy comments on the spectacle.

III.ii, 311. *You have*. Gifford reads 'you'll have', perhaps rightly.

III.iii, 44, s.d. Margaret's exit really follows the next half-line.

IV.i, 18–30. Greedy's absurd 'serious question' draws attention to the setting of the scene at Lady Alworth's house, so that when Overreach asks Lord Lovell 'How do you like this seat?' (line 66) we instantly know which house he means.

IV.i, 35–6. Marrall's speech is aside.

IV.i, 145–8. Sir Giles openly professes himself an atheist.

IV.i, 155. *Olympus*. It is really Parnassus that has a double head. But Olympus, as the unshakable seat of the gods, is obviously meant here; *cf. Julius Caesar*, III.i: 'Hence! Wilt thou lift up Olympus?' *Boreas*, line 156, the North Wind.

IV.i, 157, s.d. Amble goes first, as usher.

IV.i, 160. *Bad man*. Accented on the first syllable, *cf.* 'freeman' (III.iii, 68).

IV.i, 172–4. *Wait in the next room . . . my intents*. This makes Lady Alworth's overhearing of Overreach's words (a piece of theatrical economy) retrospectively plausible.

IV.ii, 3. *He has marr'd all*. Stress 'has', playing on his name.

IV.ii, 20. *The letter R*. For Rogue.

IV.ii, 45. *Fear me not Sir Giles*. 'Have no fear of Sir Giles.' The ethical dative: *cf. 1 Henry IV*, III.i. 'See how this river comes me cranking in'.

IV.ii, 80. *And do it before I eat*. Showing unusual resolution in a dedicated eater like Greedy; *cf. Richard III*, III.iv:
'Off with his head! Now by Saint Paul I swear I will not dine until I see the same.'

IV.ii, 82. *Unthankful knaves . . . so rewarded*. Moralizing commentary, *cf.* Marrall's departing lines, V.i, 349–50.

IV.ii, 94–5. *I was remov'd . . . stall*. 'I was forced to give up my shop and take a market stall instead.'

IV.ii, 98–100. The third creditor was 'evidently called in to cure a venereal disease'. (Spencer.)

IV.ii, 107. *And this for your respect*. To Order.

IV.iii, 50. *Though but a young actor*. Referring to herself.

IV.iii, 51, s.d. Overreach enters behind, and Margaret sees him in the middle of the following line. He is meant to overhear them from the beginning of Margaret's next speech, line 54.

IV.iii, 66–8. *I like this . . . embrac'd*. Aside.

IV.iii, 89–98. To Margaret. The repeated 'your honour'

is a good touch: it shows how skilfully Alworth is confining himself to the role of an intermediary, and it plays upon Sir Giles's desire to have his daughter 'right honourable' as soon as may be.

IV.iii, 100. *Your peevishness.* Gifford takes this as a scornful title, meaning 'you'. He may be right, after 'your honour' twice in the preceding speech.

IV.iii, 101–2. A good example of Overreach's coarseness.

IV.iii, 114. *Gotham.* Pronounced Go/–tam. A village near Nottingham.

IV.iii, 123. *I can furnish you.* Alworth's 'book' is like Hamlet's 'tables' (*Hamlet*, I.v.), a pocket notebook.

V.i, s.d. *Enter . . . Amble.* [*Exit Amble.*] Amble's entry localizes the scene at Lady Alworth's, but he cannot be present throughout it. He will re-enter with the other servants at line 144.

V.i, 22–3. *As my wishes . . . my lord.* 'As my wishes are equal with yours', taking up his last phrase.

V.i, 25. *Both a lion, and a fox.* Machiavelli's prescription for a prince's character; strong and cunning.

V.i, 73. *You are welcome sir.* Welcome also to the audience, since Lady Alworth and Lord Lovell are, it seems, ready to bandy compliments for ever.

V.i, 74. *Now you look like yourself.* In his 'rich habit' of IV.iii.

V.i, 88, s.d. So placed in Q, though most editors make Sir Giles deliver his first speech 'within'.

V.i, 90–3. Lord Lovell probably goes up stage. He has an aside at line 238, but must not, of course, be seen by Overreach, who keeps his delusion that Lord Lovell has married Margaret. He reveals himself at line 293, in Margaret's defence. He might have been expected to intervene at line 144, when the servants need to move quickly.

V.i, 105–8. Sir Giles's arrogance towards Lady Alworth forfeits any sympathy which we might feel for him in his coming disappointment; *cf.* lines 173–7.

V.i, 114. *No more?* An abrupt salutation was a mark of disrespect.

V.i, 144, s.d. *They both draw.* This first show of

violence prepares for the greater violence of Over-reach's distraction.

V.i, 185. *Indented*. 'With the crooked edge which shows where its duplicate was torn or cut off when the agreement was drawn up.' *Labels*. 'The ribbon tabs which held the seals of the parties to the agreement.' (Byrne.)

V.i, 231–3. *An army . . . Dunkirk*. Q's meaningless 'With' may result from an imperfect cancellation; compare I.ii, 127. Dunkirk was a stronghold of French pirates against whom an assault was proposed in 1625.

V.i, 361, s.d. *Flourishing his sword unsheathed*. Thus Q. Editors emend to 'sheathed' or 'ensheathed', as his sword 'will not be drawn', line 365. I have retained what I think may represent Massinger's first intention, though contradicted by the following lines, which he perhaps wrote for the sake of adding a moral point to the excitement of the scene. Alternatively, since it appears in the right-hand margin of Q, it may be merely a prompter's ill-advised suggestion. If Sir Giles has lost the use of his arm he cannot flourish his sword at all. And can anyone who is wearing a scabbard flourish a sword without drawing it?

V.i, 385. *This, th'undoubted heir*. The irregular metre suggests that a word has dropped out. Massinger perhaps wrote 'this youth, th'undoubted heir' (Alworth, as Margaret's husband, not Margaret herself, is clearly meant), disliked the two 'th' sounds, and struck out 'youth' intending to substitute another word, but never in fact did so.

V.i, 373. 'Rushes forward and flings himself on the ground.' (Gifford.)

V.i, 393. *Courses*. See I.ii, 122, for this plural form, here required by the metre.

V.i, 395. *A time of action*. In 1625 there were preparations for an English military expedition to the Continent.

V.i, 401. *But your allowance*. These words are not, of course, repeated. The epilogue begins with the half-line 400.

NOTE ON THE TEXT

THE Quarto of 1633 is the only early text of the play. It bears signs of having been printed from Massinger's own manuscript, which perhaps also served as playhouse prompt-copy before being sent to the printer.[1] Apart from some natural mistakes of the compositor it is a most reliable text, and I have followed its wording and punctuation wherever possible, altering the latter only where the original either is evidently misprinted or would positively mislead a modern reader: the reader will remember that the pointing of Jacobean plays is rather a guide to delivery than an indication of grammatical structure. I have likewise retained the elisions of the Quarto, which are very systematically marked as a guide to the metre. The act and scene headings have been changed from Latin to English, but where Latin stage directions occur they have been retained as indications of what Massinger actually wrote. The directions are throughout from the Quarto, except the few enclosed in square brackets, which are editorial, and those at the beginnings of scenes, where Massinger supplied a list of the characters taking part, with full stops between their names. The copy of the Quarto which I have used is British Museum 644.e.79.

[1] See W. J. Lawrence, 'Massinger's Punctuation' in *Those Nutcracking Elizabethans* (1935), and the note to II.iii.59 s.d. See also P. Edwards and C. Gibson, ed., *The Plays and Poems of Philip Massinger* (1976), II, 280, who agree that the copy for the Quarto was Massinger's autograph manuscript, but think it unlikely that the manuscript had been through the prompter's hands.

FURTHER READING

Stephen, L.	*Hours in a Library*, Vol. II, 1899
Cruickshank, A. H.	*Philip Massinger*, 1920
Eliot, T. S.	'Philip Massinger', *Selected Essays*, 1934
Chelli, M.	*Le Drame de Massinger*, 1924
Knights, L. C.	*Drama and Society in the Age of Jonson*, 1937
Ball, R. H.	*The Amazing Career of Sir Giles Overreach*, 1939
Enright, D. J.	'Poetic Satire and Satire in Verse', *Scrutiny*, XVIII, 1952
Dunn, T. A.	*Philip Massinger*, 1952
Leggatt, A.	*Citizen Comedy in the Age of Shakespeare*, 1973
Gibbons, B.	*Jacobean City Comedy*, 1968 (new ed. 1980)

The introductions to the editions cited in the *Acknowledgements* are also recommended.

Printed in Great Britain by Fakenham Press Limited
Fakenham, Norfolk